ALSO BY JOHN GRAY

Mill on Liberty: A Defense

Conceptions of Liberty in Political Philosophy (ed. with Zbigniew Pelczynski)

Hayek on Liberty

Liberalism

Liberalisms: Essays in Political Philosophy

J. S. Mill, "On Liberty": In Focus (ed. with G. W. Smith)

Beyond the New Right: Markets, Government and the Common Environment

Post-liberalism: Studies in Political Thought

Enlightenment's Wake: Politics and Culture at the Close of the Modern Age

Isaiah Berlin

After Social Democracy: Politics, Capitalism and the Common Life

Endgames: Questions in Late Modern Political Thought

False Dawn: The Delusions of Global Capitalism

Voltaire

Two Faces of Liberalism

Al Qaeda and What It Means to Be Modern

Heresies: Against Progress and Other Illusions

Black Mass: Apocalyptic Religion and the Death of Utopia

STRAW DOGS

STRAW DOGS

THOUGHTS ON HUMANS

AND OTHER ANIMALS

JOHN GRAY

FARRAR, STRAUS AND GIROUX

NEW YORK

Farrar, Straus and Giroux
18 West 18th Street, New York 10011

Owing to limitations of space, all acknowledgments for permission to reprint
previously published material can be found on page 247.

Library of Congress Cataloging-in-Publication Data
Gray, John, 1948–
     Straw dogs : thoughts on humans and other animals / John Gray.— 1st
American ed.
        p.   cm.
     Includes index.
     ISBN-13: 978-0-374-27093-3 (pbk. : alk. paper)
     ISBN-10: 0-374-27093-7 (pbk. : alk. paper)
     1. Humanism.   I. Title.

B821 .G72 2007
128—dc22

                                                    2007012936

www.fsgbooks.com

11

Heaven and earth are ruthless, and treat the myriad creatures as straw dogs.

LAO TZU

CONTENTS

ACKNOWLEDGEMENTS

In this book I have tried to present a view of things in which humans are not central. My thoughts are presented in fragments, but they are not unsystematic. I hope they can be read one after the other, or dipped into at will. I have made rather extensive use of quotations – not, I believe, in order to lend authority to an unfamiliar way of thinking, but simply to illustrate what it might mean. The notes at the back of the book have the same aim.

Several people have given me stimulus, advice and encouragement. Exchanges with James Lovelock helped clarify my thinking on the Gaia hypothesis. Reading and talking with J. G. Ballard sharpened my view of the present and the near future. Adam Phillips's comments and suggestions on a draft version have shaped the book in a number of ways. Simon May gave me detailed comments on the philosophical portions, and Vincent Deary gave me comments on the sections of the book dealing with consciousness. At Granta, Neil Belton gave me unfailing encouragement and advice, and Sara Holloway gave me invaluable comments and suggestions all the way through the book's gestation and production. I owe debts to all of these people, but I have not always followed any advice they may have given. Responsibility for the thoughts expressed here remains mine.

The book is dedicated to Mieko, without whom it would not have been written.

FOREWORD TO THE
PAPERBACK EDITION

Straw Dogs is an attack on the unthinking beliefs of thinking people. Today liberal humanism has the pervasive power that was once possessed by revealed religion. Humanists like to think they have a rational view of the world; but their core belief in progress is a superstition, further from the truth about the human animal than any of the world's religions.

Outside of science, progress is simply a myth. In some readers of *Straw Dogs* this observation seems to have produced a moral panic. Surely, they ask, no one can question the central article of faith of liberal societies? Without it, will we not despair? Like trembling Victorians terrified of losing their faith, these humanists cling to the moth-eaten brocade of progressive hope. Today religious believers are more free-thinking. Driven to the margins of a culture in which science claims authority over all of human knowledge, they have had to cultivate a capacity for doubt. In contrast, secular believers – held fast by the conventional wisdom of the time – are in the grip of unexamined dogmas.

The prevailing secular worldview is a pastiche of current scientific orthodoxy and pious hopes. Darwin has shown that we are animals; but – as humanists never tire of preaching – how we live is 'up to us'. Unlike any other animal, we are told, we are free to live as we choose. Yet the idea of free will does not come from science. Its origins are in religion – not just any religion, but the Christian faith against which humanists rail so obsessively.

In the ancient world the Epicureans speculated about the possibility that some events may be uncaused; but the belief that humans are marked off from all other animals by having free will is a Christian inheritance. Darwin's theory would not have caused such a scandal had it been formulated in Hindu India, Taoist China or animist Africa. Equally, it is only in post-Christian cultures that philosophers labour so piously to reconcile scientific determinism with a belief in the unique capacity of humans to choose the way they live. The irony of evangelical Darwinism is that it uses science to support a view of humanity that comes from religion.

Some readers have seen *Straw Dogs* as an attempt to apply Darwinism to ethics and politics, but nowhere does it suggest that neo-Darwinian orthodoxy contains the final account of the human animal. Instead Darwinism is deployed strategically in order to break up the prevailing humanist worldview. Humanists turn to Darwin to support their shaky modern faith in progress; but there is no progress in the world he revealed. A truly naturalistic view of the world leaves no room for secular hope.

Among contemporary philosophers it is a matter of pride to be ignorant of theology. As a result, the Christian origins of secular humanism are rarely understood. Yet they were perfectly clear to its founders. In the early nineteenth century the French Positivists Henri Saint-Simon and Auguste Comte invented the Religion of Humanity, a vision of a universal civilization based on science that is the prototype for the political religions of the twentieth century. Through their impact on John Stuart Mill, they made liberalism the secular creed it is today. Through their deep influence on Karl Marx, they helped shape 'scientific socialism'. Ironically, for Saint-Simon and Comte were fierce critics of *laissez-faire* economics, they also inspired the late-twentieth-century cult of the global free market. I have told this paradoxical and often farcical story in my book *Al Qaeda and What It Means to Be Modern*.

Humanism is not science, but religion – the post-Christian faith that humans can make a world better than any in which they have so far lived. In pre-Christian Europe it was taken for granted that the future would be like the past. Knowledge and invention might advance, but ethics would remain much the same. History was a series of cycles, with no overall meaning.

Against this pagan view, Christians understood history as a story of sin and redemption. Humanism is the transformation of this Christian doctrine of salvation into a project of universal human emancipation. The idea of progress is a secular version of the Christian belief in providence. That is why among the ancient pagans it was unknown.

Belief in progress has another source. In science, the growth of knowledge is cumulative. But human life as a whole is not a cumulative activity; what is gained in one generation may be lost in the next. In science, knowledge is an unmixed good; in ethics and politics it is bad as well as good. Science increases human power – and magnifies the flaws in human nature. It enables us to live longer and have higher living standards than in the past. At the same time it allows us to wreak destruction – on each other and the Earth – on a larger scale than ever before.

The idea of progress rests on the belief that the growth of knowledge and the advance of the species go together – if not now, then in the long run. The biblical myth of the Fall of Man contains the forbidden truth. Knowledge does not make us free. It leaves us as we have always been, prey to every kind of folly. The same truth is found in Greek myth. The punishment of Prometheus, chained to a rock for stealing fire from the gods, was not unjust.

If the hope of progress is an illusion, how – it will be asked – are we to live? The question assumes that humans can live well only if they believe they have the power to remake the world. Yet most humans who have ever lived have not believed this – and a great many have had happy lives. The question assumes the aim of life is action; but this is a modern heresy. For Plato contemplation was the highest form of human activity. A similar view existed in ancient India. The aim of life was not to change the world. It was to see it rightly.

Today this is a subversive truth, for it entails the vanity of politics. Good politics is shabby and makeshift, but at the start of the twenty-first century the world is strewn with the grandiose ruins of failed utopias. With the Left moribund, the Right has become the home of the utopian imagination. Global communism has been followed by global capitalism. The two visions of the future have much in common. Both are hideous and fortunately chimerical.

Political action has come to be a surrogate for salvation; but no political project can deliver humanity from its natural condition. However radical, political programmes are expedients – modest devices for coping with recurring evils. Hegel writes somewhere that humanity will be content only when it lives in a world of its own making. In contrast, *Straw Dogs* argues for a shift from human solipsism. Humans cannot save the world, but this is no reason for despair. It does not need saving. Happily, humans will never live in a world of their own making.

John Gray, May 2003

1
THE HUMAN

All religions, nearly all philosophies, and even a part of science testify to the unwearying, heroic effort of mankind desperately denying its contingency.

JACQUES MONOD

1

SCIENCE VERSUS HUMANISM

Most people today think they belong to a species that can be master of its destiny. This is faith, not science. We do not speak of a time when whales or gorillas will be masters of their destinies. Why then humans?

We do not need Darwin to see that we belong with other animals. A little observation of our lives soon leads to the same conclusion. Still, since science has today an authority that common experience cannot rival, let us note that Darwin teaches that species are only assemblies of genes, interacting at random with each other and their shifting environments. Species cannot control their fates. Species do not exist. This applies equally to humans. Yet it is forgotten whenever people talk of 'the progress of mankind'. They have put their faith in an abstraction that no one would think of taking seriously if it were not formed from cast-off Christian hopes.

If Darwin's discovery had been made in a Taoist or Shinto, Hindu or animist, culture it would very likely have become just one more strand in its intertwining mythologies.

In these faiths humans and other animals are kin. By contrast, arising among Christians who set humans beyond all other living things, it triggered a bitter controversy that rages on to this day. In Victorian times this was a conflict between Christians and unbelievers. Today it is waged between humanists and the few who understand that humans can no more be masters of their destiny than any other animal.

Humanism can mean many things, but for us it means belief in progress. To believe in progress is to believe that, by using the new powers given us by growing scientific knowledge, humans can free themselves from the limits that frame the lives of other animals. This is the hope of nearly everybody nowadays, but it is groundless. For though human knowledge will very likely continue to grow and with it human power, the human animal will stay the same: a highly inventive species that is also one of the most predatory and destructive.

Darwin showed that humans are like other animals, humanists claim they are not. Humanists insist that by using our knowledge we can control our environment and flourish as never before. In affirming this, they renew one of Christianity's most dubious promises – that salvation is open to all. The humanist belief in progress is only a secular version of this Christian faith.

In the world shown us by Darwin, there is nothing that can be called progress. To anyone reared on humanist hopes this is intolerable. As a result, Darwin's teaching has been stood on its head, and Christianity's cardinal error – that humans are different from all other animals – has been given a new lease on life.

4

2

THE MIRAGE OF CONSCIOUS EVOLUTION

Humans are the most adventitious of creatures – a result of blind evolutionary drift. Yet, with the power of genetic engineering, we need no longer be ruled by chance. Humankind – so we are told – can shape its own future.

According to E. O. Wilson, conscious control of human evolution is not only possible but inevitable:

> ... genetic evolution is about to become conscious and volitional, and usher in a new epoch in the history of life. ... The prospect of this 'volitional evolution' – a species deciding what to do about its own heredity – will present the most profound intellectual and ethical choices humanity has ever faced ... humanity will be positioned godlike to take control of its own ultimate fate. It can, if it chooses, alter not just the anatomy and intelligence of the species but also the emotions and creative drive that compose the very core of human nature.

The author of this passage is the greatest contemporary Darwinian. He has been attacked by biologists and social scientists who believe that the human species is not governed by the same laws as other animals. In that war Wilson is undoubtedly on the side of truth. Yet the prospect of conscious human evolution he invokes is a mirage. The idea of humanity taking charge of its destiny makes sense only if we ascribe consciousness and purpose to the species; but Darwin's discovery was that species are only currents in the drift of genes. The idea that humanity can shape its future assumes that it is exempt from this truth.

It seems feasible that over the coming century human nature will be scientifically remodelled. If so, it will be done haphazardly, as an upshot of struggles in the murky realm where big business, organised crime and the hidden parts of government vie for control. If the human species is re-engineered it will not be the result of humanity assuming a godlike control of its destiny. It will be another twist in man's fate.

3

DISSEMINATED PRIMATEMAIA

James Lovelock has written:

> Humans on the Earth behave in some ways like a pathogenic organism, or like the cells of a tumour or neoplasm. We have grown in numbers and disturbance to Gaia, to the point where our presence is perceptibly disturbing . . . the human species is now so numerous as to constitute a serious planetary malady. Gaia is suffering from *Disseminated Primatemaia*, a plague of people.

Around 65 million years ago the dinosaurs and three quarters of all other species suddenly perished. The cause is disputed, but many scientists believe the mass extinction was the result of a meteorite colliding with the Earth. Today species are disappearing at a rate that is set to surpass that last great extinction. The cause is not any cosmic catastrophe. As Lovelock says, it is a plague of people.

'Darwin's dice have rolled badly for Earth,' Wilson points out. The lucky throw that brought the human species to its present power has meant ruin for countless other life forms. When humans arrived in the New World around twelve thousand years ago, the continent abounded in mammoths, mastodons, camels, giant ground sloths and dozens of similar species. Most of these indigenous species were hunted to extinction. North America lost over 70 per cent and South America 80 per cent of its large mammals, according to Diamond.

The destruction of the natural world is not the result of global capitalism, industrialisation, 'Western civilisation' or any flaw in human institutions. It is a consequence of the evolutionary success of an exceptionally rapacious primate. Throughout all of history and prehistory, human advance has coincided with ecological devastation.

It is true that a few traditional peoples lived in balance with the Earth for long periods. The Inuit and the Bushmen stumbled into ways of life in which their footprint was slight. We cannot tread the Earth so lightly. *Homo rapiens* has become too numerous.

The study of population is not a very exact science. No one forecast the population collapse that is occurring in post-communist European Russia, or the scale of the fall in fertility that is under way in much of the world. The margin of error in calculations of fertility and life expectancy is large. Even so, a further large increase is inevitable. As Morrison observes, 'Even if we assume a declining birth rate due to social factors and a rising death rate due to starvation, disease and genocide, the present global population of over 6 billion will grow by at least 1.2 billion by the year 2050.'

A human population of approaching 8 billion can be maintained only by desolating the Earth. If wild habitat is given over to human cultivation and habitation, if rainforests can be turned into green deserts, if genetic engineering enables ever-higher yields to be extorted from the thinning soils – then humans will have created for themselves a new geological era, the Eremozoic, the Era of Solitude, in which little remains on the Earth but themselves and the prosthetic environment that keeps them alive.

It is a hideous vision, but it is only a nightmare. Either the Earth's self-regulating mechanisms will make the planet less habitable for humans or the side effects of their own activities will cut short the current growth in their numbers.

Lovelock suggests four possible outcomes of *disseminated primatemaia*: 'destruction of the invading disease organisms; chronic infection; destruction of the host; or symbiosis – a lasting relationship of mutual benefit to the host and invader'.

Of the four outcomes, the last is the least likely. Humanity will never initiate a symbiosis with the Earth. Even so, it will not destroy its planetary host, Lovelock's third possible outcome. The biosphere is older and stronger than they will ever be. As Margulis writes, 'No human culture, despite its inventiveness, can kill life on this planet, were it even to try.'

Nor can humans chronically infect their host. True, human activity is already altering the planetary balance. The production of greenhouse gases has changed global ecosystems irreversibly. With worldwide industrialisation, such changes can only accelerate. In a worst-case scenario that some scientists are taking seriously, climate change could wipe out populous coastal countries such as Bangladesh and trigger agricultural failure in other parts of the world, spelling disaster for billions of people, before the end of the present century.

The scale of the change afoot cannot be known with certainty. In a chaotic system even the near future cannot be predicted accurately. Yet it seems likely that the conditions of life are shifting for much of humankind, with large segments of it facing much less hospitable climates. As Lovelock has suggested, climate change may be a mechanism through which the planet eases its human burden.

As a side effect of climate change, new patterns of disease could trim the human population. Our bodies are bacterial communities, linked indissolubly with a largely bacterial biosphere. Epidemiology and microbiology are better guides to our future than any of our hopes or plans.

War could have a major impact. Writing at the turn of the nineteenth century, Thomas Malthus named war as being one of the ways – along with recurrent famines – in which population and resources were kept in balance. Malthus's argument was satirised in the twentieth century by Leonard C. Lewin:

Man, like all other animals, is subject to the continuing process of adapting to the limitations of his environment. But the principal mechanism he has utilised for this purpose is unique among living creatures. To forestall the inevitable historical cycles of inadequate food supply, post-Neolithic man destroys surplus members of his own species by organised warfare.

The irony is misplaced. War has rarely resulted in any long-term reduction of human numbers. Yet today its impact could be considerable. It is not only that weapons of mass destruction – notably biological and (soon) genetic weapons – are more fearsome than before. More, their impact on the life-support systems of human society is likely to be greater. A globalised world is a delicate construction. A vastly greater population than hitherto is dependent on far-flung supply networks, and any war on the scale of the larger conflicts of the twentieth century could have the effect of culling the population in the way Malthus described.

In 1600 the human population was about half a billion. In the 1990s it increased by the same amount. People who are now over forty have lived through a doubling of the world's human population. It is natural for them to think that these numbers will be maintained. Natural, but – unless humans really are different from all other animals – mistaken.

The human population growth that has taken place over the past few hundred years resembles nothing so much as the spikes that occur in the numbers of rabbits, house mice and plague rats. Like them, it can only be short-lived. Already fertility is falling throughout much of the world. As Morrison observes, humans are like other animals in responding to stress. They react to scarcity and overcrowding by tuning down the reproductive urge:

> Many other animals seem to have a hormone-regulated response to environmental stress that switches their metabolism into a more economical mode whenever resources become scarce. Inevitably, the energy-hungry processes of reproduction are the first to be targeted. . . . The telltale hormonal signature of this process . . . has been identified in captive lowland gorillas, and in women.

In responding to environmental stress by ceasing to breed, humans are no different from other mammals.

The current spike in human numbers may come to an end for any number of reasons – climate change, new patterns of disease, the side effects of war, a downward spiral in the birth rate, or a mix of these and other, unknown factors. Whatever brings about its end, it is an aberration:

> . . . if the human plague is really as normal as it looks, then the collapse curve should mirror the population growth curve. This means that the bulk of the collapse will not take much more than one hundred years, and by the year 2150 the biosphere should be safely back to its preplague population of Homo sapiens – somewhere between 0.5 and 1 billion.

Humans are like any other plague animal. They cannot destroy the Earth, but they can easily wreck the environment that sustains them. The most likely of Lovelock's four outcomes is a version of the first, in which *disseminated primatemaia* is cured by a large-scale decline in human numbers.

4

WHY HUMANITY WILL NEVER MASTER TECHNOLOGY

'Humanity' does not exist. There are only humans, driven by conflicting needs and illusions, and subject to every kind of infirmity of will and judgement.

At present there are nearly two hundred sovereign states in the world. Most are unstable, oscillating between weak democracy and weak tyranny; many are rusted through with corruption, or controlled by organised crime; whole regions of the world – much of Africa, southern Asia, Russia, the Balkans and the Caucasus, and parts of South America – are strewn with corroded or collapsed states. At the same time, the world's most powerful states – the United States, China and Japan – will not accept any fundamental limitation on their sovereignty. They are jealous of their freedom of action, if only because they have been enemies in the past and know they may become so again in the future.

Yet it is not the number of sovereign states that makes technology ungovernable. It is technology itself. The ability to design new viruses for use in genocidal weapons does not require enormous resources of money, plant or equipment. New technologies of mass destruction are cheap; the knowledge they embody is free. It is impossible to prevent them becoming ever more easily available.

Bill Joy, one of the pioneers of the new information technologies, has written thus:

> The 21st century technologies – genetics, nanotechnologies and robotics – are so powerful that they can spawn whole new classes of accidents and abuses. Most dangerously, for the first time, these accidents and abuses are widely within the reach of individuals or small groups. They will not require large facilities or rare raw materials. Knowledge alone will enable the use of them. Thus we have the possibility not just of weapons of mass destruction but of knowledge-enabled mass destruction (KMD), this destructiveness hugely amplified by the power of self-replication.

In part, governments have created this situation. By ceding so much control over new technology to the marketplace they have colluded in their own powerlessness. Nevertheless, the proliferation of new weapons of mass destruction is not in the end a result of errors in policy. It is a consequence of the diffusion of knowledge.

Controls on technology cannot be enforced. The genetic modification of crops, animals or humans may be forbidden in some countries, but it will go ahead in others. The world's powers can pledge that genetic engineering will have only benign uses, but it can be only a matter of time before it is used for purposes of war. Perhaps the world's most unstable states can be prevented from acquiring nuclear capability. But how can biological weapons be kept out of the hands of forces no government controls?

If anything about the present century is certain, it is that the power conferred on 'humanity' by new technologies will be used to commit atrocious crimes against it. If it becomes possible to clone human beings, soldiers will be bred in whom normal human emotions are stunted or absent. Genetic engineering may enable age-old diseases to be eradicated. At the same time, it is likely to be the technology of choice in future genocides.

Those who ignore the destructive potential of new technologies can do so only because they ignore history. Pogroms are as old as Christendom; but without railways, the telegraph and poison gas there could have been no Holocaust. There have always been tyrannies; but without modern means of transport and communication, Stalin and Mao could not have built their gulags. Humanity's worst crimes were made possible only by modern technology.

There is a deeper reason why 'humanity' will never control technology. Technology is not something that humankind can control. It is an event that has befallen the world.

Once a technology enters human life – whether it be fire, the wheel, the automobile, radio, television or the Internet – it changes it in ways we can never fully understand. Cars may have been invented to make moving about easier; but they soon came to be embodiments of forbidden desires. According to Illich, 'The model American puts in 1,600 hours to get 7,500 miles: less than five miles an hour' – not much more than he could travel on his own feet. Which is more important today: the use of cars as means of transportation, or their use as expressions of our unconscious yearnings for personal freedom, sexual release and the final liberation of sudden death?

Nothing is more commonplace than to lament that moral progress has failed to keep pace with scientific knowledge. If only we were more intelligent or more moral, we could use technology only for benign ends. The fault is not in our tools, we say, but in ourselves.

In one sense this is true. Technical progress leaves only one problem unsolved: the frailty of human nature. Unfortunately that problem is insoluble.

5

GREEN HUMANISM

Green thinkers understand that humans can never be masters of the Earth. Yet in their Luddite struggle against technology they renew the illusion that the world can be made the instrument of human purposes. Whatever they say, most Green thinkers offer yet another version of humanism, not an alternative to it.

Technology is not a human artefact: it is as old as life on Earth. As Brian J. Ford notes, it is found in the kingdom of insects:

The industry undertaken by some leaf-cutter ants is close to farming. They excavate large underground nests which the colony inhabits. Workers go out foraging for leaves which they cut with their jaws and bring back to the nest. These leaves are used to grow colonies of fungi, enzymes from which can digest the cellulose cell walls of the leaves and render them suitable for eating by the colony. . . . The garden is vital for the ants' survival; without the continuous farming and feeding of the fungal colonies, the ant colony is doomed. These ants are indulging in an agricultural enterprise which they systematically maintain.

Cities are no more artificial than the hives of bees. The Internet is as natural as a spider's web. As Margulis and Sagan have written, we are ourselves technological devices, invented by ancient bacterial communities as means of genetic survival: 'We are a part of an intricate network that comes from the original bacterial takeover of the Earth. Our powers and intelligence do not belong specifically to us but to all life.' Thinking of our bodies as natural and of our technologies as artificial gives too much importance to the accident of our origins. If we are replaced by machines, it will be in an evolutionary shift no different from that when bacteria combined to create our earliest ancestors.

Humanism is a doctrine of salvation – the belief that humankind can take charge of its destiny. Among Greens, this has become the ideal of humanity becoming the wise steward of the planet's resources. But for anyone whose hopes are not centred on their own species the notion that human action can save themselves or the planet must be absurd. They know the upshot is not in human hands. They act as they do not out of the belief that they can succeed, but from an ancient instinct.

For much of their history and all of prehistory, humans did not see themselves as being any different from the other animals among which they lived. Hunter-gatherers saw their prey as equals, if not superiors, and animals were worshipped as divinities in many traditional cultures. The humanist sense of a gulf between ourselves and other animals is an aberration. It is the animist feeling of belonging with the rest of nature that is normal. Feeble as it may be today, the feeling of sharing a common destiny with other living things is embedded in the human psyche. Those who struggle to conserve what is left of the environment are moved by the love of living things, *biophilia*, the frail bond of feeling that ties humankind to the Earth.

The mass of mankind is ruled not by its intermittent moral sensations, still less by self-interest, but by the needs of the moment. It seems fated to wreck the balance of life on Earth – and thereby to be the agent of its own destruction. What could be more hopeless than placing the Earth in the charge of this exceptionally destructive species? It is not of becoming the planet's wise stewards that Earth-lovers dream, but of a time when humans have ceased to matter.

6

AGAINST FUNDAMENTALISM – RELIGIOUS AND SCIENTIFIC

Religious fundamentalists see the power of science as the chief source of modern disenchantment. Science has supplanted religion as the chief source of authority, but at the cost of making human life accidental and insignificant. If our lives are to have any meaning, the power of science must be overthrown, and faith re-established. But science cannot be removed from our lives by an act of will. Its power flows from technology, which is changing the way we live regardless of what we will.

Religious fundamentalists see themselves as having remedies for the maladies of the modern world. In reality they are symptoms of the disease they pretend to cure. They hope to recover the unreflective faith of traditional cultures, but this is a peculiarly modern fantasy. We cannot believe as we please; our beliefs are traces left by our unchosen lives. A view of the world is not something that can be conjured up as and when we please. Once gone, traditional ways of life cannot be retrieved. Whatever we contrive in their wake merely adds to the clamour of incessant novelty. However much they may wish it, people whose lives are veined through with science cannot return to a pre-scientific outlook.

Scientific fundamentalists claim that science is the disinterested pursuit of truth. But representing science in this way is to disregard the human needs science serves. Among us, science serves two needs: for hope and censorship. Today, only science supports the myth of progress. If people cling to the hope of progress, it is not so much from genuine belief as from fear of what may come if they give it up. The political projects of the twentieth century have failed, or achieved much less than they promised. At the same time, progress in science is a daily experience, confirmed whenever we buy a new electronic gadget, or take a new drug. Science gives us a sense of progress that ethical and political life cannot.

Again, science alone has the power to silence heretics. Today it is the only institution that can claim authority. Like the Church in the past, it has the power to destroy, or marginalise, independent thinkers. (Think how orthodox medicine reacted to Freud, and orthodox Darwinians to Lovelock.) In fact, science does not yield any fixed picture of things, but by censoring thinkers who stray too far from current orthodoxies it preserves the comforting illusion of a single established worldview. From the standpoint of anyone who values freedom of thought, this may be unfortunate, but it is undoubtedly the chief source of science's appeal. For us, science is a refuge from uncertainty, promising – and in some measure delivering – the miracle of freedom from thought; while churches have become sanctuaries for doubt.

Bertrand Russell – a defender of science wiser than its ideologues today – had this to say:

When I speak of the importance of scientific method in regard to the conduct of human life, I am thinking of scientific method in its mundane forms. Not that I would undervalue science as a metaphysic, but the value of science as metaphysic belongs in another sphere. It belongs with religion and art and love, with the pursuit of the beatific vision, with the Promethean madness that leads the greatest men to strive to become gods. Perhaps the only ultimate value of human life is to be found in this Promethean madness. But it is a value that is religious, not political, or even moral.

The authority of science comes from the power it gives humans over their environment. Now and then, perhaps, science can cut loose from our practical needs, and serve the pursuit of truth. But to think that it can ever embody that quest is pre-scientific – it is to detach science from human needs, and make of it something that is not natural but transcendental. To think of science as the search for truth is to renew a mystical faith, the faith of Plato and Augustine, that truth rules the world, that truth is divine.

7

SCIENCE'S IRRATIONAL ORIGINS

As portrayed by its fundamentalists, science is the supreme expression of reason. They tell us that if it rules our lives today, it is only after a long struggle in which it was ceaselessly opposed by the Church, the state and every kind of irrational belief. Having arisen in the struggle against superstition, science – they say – has become the embodiment of rational inquiry.

This fairy tale conceals a more interesting history. The origins of science are not in rational inquiry but in faith, magic and trickery. Modern science triumphed over its adversaries not through its superior rationality but because its late-medieval and early-modern founders were more skilful than them in the use of rhetoric and the arts of politics.

Galileo did not win in his campaign for Copernican astronomy because he conformed to any precept of 'scientific method'. As Feyerabend argued, he prevailed because of his persuasive skill – and because he wrote in Italian. By writing in Italian rather than Latin, Galileo was able to identify resistance to Copernican astronomy with the bankrupt scholasticism of his time, and so gain support from people opposed to older traditions of learning: 'Copernicus now stands for progress in other areas as well, he is a symbol for the ideals of a new class that looks back to the classical times of Plato and Cicero and forward to a free and pluralistic society.'

Galileo won out not because he had the best arguments but because he was able to represent the new astronomy as part of a coming trend in society. His success illustrates a crucial truth. To limit the practice of science by rules of method would slow the growth of knowledge, or even halt it:

> The difference between science and methodology which is such an obvious fact of history . . . indicates a weakness in the latter, and perhaps of the 'laws of reason' as

well. . . . Without 'chaos', no knowledge. Without a frequent dismissal of reason, no progress. Ideas which today form the very basis of science exist because there were such things as prejudice, conceit, passion; because these things *opposed reason*; and because they *were permitted to have their way*.

According to the most influential twentieth-century philosopher of science, Karl Popper, a theory is scientific only in so far as it is falsifiable, and should be given up as soon as it has been falsified. By this standard, the theories of Darwin and Einstein should never have been accepted. When they were first advanced, each of them was at odds with some available evidence; only later did evidence become available that gave them crucial support. Applying Popper's account of scientific method would have killed these theories at birth.

The greatest scientists have never been bound by what are now regarded as the rules of scientific method. Nor did the philosophies of the founders of modern science – magical and metaphysical, mystical and occult – have much in common with what is today taken to be the scientific worldview. Galileo saw himself as a defender of theology, not as an enemy of the Church. Newton's theories became the basis for a mechanistic philosophy, but in his own mind his theories were inseparable from a religious conception of the world as a divinely created order. Newton explained apparently anomalous occurrences as traces left by God. Tycho Brahe viewed them as miracles. Johannes Kepler described anomalies in astronomy as reactions of 'the telluric soul'. As Feyerabend observes, beliefs that are today regarded as belonging to religion, myth or magic were central in the worldviews of the people who originated modern science.

As pictured by philosophers, science is a supremely rational activity. Yet the history of science shows scientists flouting the rules of scientific method. Not only the origins but the progress of science comes from acting against reason.

8

SCIENCE AS A REMEDY FOR ANTHROPOCENTRISM

In all its practical uses, science works to entrench anthropocentrism. It encourages us to believe that, unlike any other animal, we can understand the natural world, and thereby bend it to our will.

Yet, in fact, science suggests a view of things that is intensely uncomfortable to the human mind. The world as seen by physicists such as Erwin Schrödinger and Werner Heisenberg is not an orderly cosmos. It is a demi-chaos that humans can hope to understand only in part. Science cannot satisfy the human need to find order in the world. The most advanced physical sciences suggest that causality and classical logic may not be built into the nature of things. Even the most basic features of our ordinary experience may be delusive.

The passage of time is an integral part of everyday life. Yet, as Barbour points out, science suggests that time may not be part of the scheme of things. Classical logic tells us that the same event cannot happen and not happen. Yet, in 'many-worlds' interpretations of modern physics, that is precisely what does occur. It has become part of common sense to believe that the physical world is not changed by the fact that we observe it. But the alteration of the world by its observers is at the core of quantum mechanics. Like technology, science has evolved to meet human needs; again like technology, it discloses a world humans cannot control, or ever fully understand.

Science has been used to support the conceit that humans are unlike all other animals in their ability to understand the world. In fact, its supreme value may be in showing that the world humans are programmed to perceive is a chimera.

9

TRUTH AND CONSEQUENCES

Humanists believe that if we know the truth we will be free. In affirming this they imagine they are wiser than thinkers of earlier times. In fact they are in the grip of a forgotten religion.

The modern faith in truth is a relic of an ancient creed. Socrates founded European thought on the faith that truth makes us free. He never doubted that knowledge and the good life go together. He passed on this faith to Plato, and so to Christianity. The result is modern humanism.

Socrates was able to believe that the examined life is best because he thought the true and the good were one and the same: there is a changeless reality beyond the visible world, and it is perfect. When humans live the unexamined life they run after illusions. They spend their lives searching for pleasure or fleeing pain, both of which are bound to pass away. True fulfilment lies in changeless things. An examined life is best because it leads us into eternity.

We need not doubt the reality of truth to reject this Socratic faith. Human knowledge is one thing, human well-being another. There is no predetermined harmony between the two. The examined life may not be worth living.

The faith of Socrates in the examined life may well have been a trace of an archaic religion: he 'habitually heard and obeyed an inner voice which knew more than he did . . . he called it, quite simply, "the voice of God"'. Socrates was guided by a *daimon*, an inner oracle, whose counsels he followed without question, even when they led him to his death. In admitting that he was guided by an inner voice, he showed the lingering power of shamanic practices, in which humans have immemorially sought communion with spirits.

If Socratic philosophy originates in shamanism, European rationalism was born in a mystical experience. Modern humanism differs from Socratic philosophy chiefly in failing to recognise its irrational origins – and in the hubris of its ambitions.

The bequest of Socrates was to tether the pursuit of truth to a mystical ideal of the good. Yet neither Socrates nor any other ancient thinker imagined that truth could make *mankind* free. They took for granted that freedom would always remain the privilege of a few; there was no hope for the species. By contrast, among contemporary humanists, the Greek faith that truth makes us free has been fused with one of Christianity's most dubious legacies – the belief that the hope of freedom belongs to everyone.

Modern humanism is the faith that through science humankind can know the truth – and so be free. But if Darwin's theory of natural selection is true this is impossible. The human mind serves evolutionary success, not truth. To think otherwise is to resurrect the pre-Darwinian error that humans are different from all other animals.

An example is the theory of memes. Memes are clusters of ideas and beliefs, which are supposed to compete with one another in much the same way that genes do. In the life of the mind, as in biological evolution, there is a kind of natural selection of memes, whereby the fittest memes survive. Unfortunately, memes are not genes. There is no mechanism of selection in the history of ideas akin to that of the natural selection of genetic mutations in evolution.

In any case, only someone miraculously innocent of history could believe that competition among ideas could result in the triumph of truth. Certainly ideas compete with one another, but the winners are normally those with power and human folly on their side. When the medieval Church exterminated the Cathars, did Catholic memes prevail over the memes of the heretics? If the Final Solution had been carried to a conclusion, would that have demonstrated the inferiority of Hebrew memes?

Darwinian theory tells us that an interest in truth is not needed for survival or reproduction. More often it is a disadvantage. Deception is common among primates and birds. As Heinrich observes, ravens pretend to hide a cache of food, while secreting it somewhere else. Evolutionary psychologists have shown that deceit is pervasive in animal communication. Among humans the best deceivers are those who deceive themselves: 'we deceive ourselves in order to deceive others better', says Wright. A lover who promises eternal fidelity is more likely to be believed if he believes his promise himself; he is no more likely to keep the promise. In a competition for mates, a well-developed capacity for self-deception is an advantage. The same is true in politics, and many other contexts.

If this is so, the view that clusters of false beliefs – inferior memes – will tend to be winnowed out by natural selection must be mistaken. Truth has no systematic evolutionary advantage over error. Quite to the contrary, evolution will 'select for a degree of self-deception, rendering some facts and motives unconscious so as not to betray – by the subtle signs of self-knowledge – the deception being practised'. As Trivers points out, evolution favours useful error: 'the conventional view that natural selection favours nervous systems which produce ever more accurate images of the world must be a very naive view of mental evolution'.

In the struggle for life, a taste for truth is a luxury – or else a disability:

only

tormented persons want truth.

Man is like other animals, wants food and success and
    women,

not truth. Only if the mind

Tortured by some interior tension has despaired of
    happiness:

then it hates

its life-cage and seeks further.

Science will never be used chiefly to pursue truth, or to
improve human life. The uses of knowledge will always be as
shifting and crooked as humans are themselves. Humans use
what they know to meet their most urgent needs – even if the
result is ruin. History is not made in the struggle for self-
preservation, as Hobbes imagined or wished to believe. In
their everyday lives humans struggle to reckon profit and loss.
When times are desperate they act to protect their offspring,
to revenge themselves on enemies, or simply to give vent to
their feelings.

These are not flaws that can be remedied. Science cannot
be used to reshape humankind in a more rational mould. Any
new-model humanity will only reproduce the familiar defor-
mities of its designers. It is a strange fancy to suppose that
science can bring reason to an irrational world, when all it can
ever do is give another twist to the normal madness. These are
not just inferences from history. The upshot of scientific inquiry
is that humans cannot be other than irrational. Curiously, this
is a conclusion few rationalists have been ready to accept.

Tertullian, a theologian who lived in Carthage sometime around A.D. 200, wrote of Christianity: *Certum est, quia impossible* (it is certain because it is impossible). Humanists are less clear-minded, but their faith is just as irrational. They do not deny that history is a catalogue of unreason, but their remedy is simple: humankind must – and will – be reasonable. Without this absurd, Tertullian-like faith, the Enlightenment is a gospel of despair.

10

A PASCAL FOR THE ENLIGHTENMENT

Humans cannot live without illusion. For the men and women of today, an irrational faith in progress may be the only antidote to nihilism. Without the hope that the future will be better than the past, they could not go on. In that case, we may need a latter-day Pascal.

The great seventeenth-century religious thinker found many reasons for belief, but he never imagined that they could instil faith. Instead he counselled that reason be stupefied. Pascal knew that faith rests on the force of habit: 'we must make no mistake about ourselves: we are as much automaton as mind'. Only by submitting to the Church and taking Mass with believers could doubt be stilled.

By submitting to the authority of science we can hope for a similar freedom from thought. By revering scientists and partaking of their gifts of technology, we can achieve what

Pascal hoped for from prayer, incense and holy water. By seeking the company of earnest investigators and intelligent machines, we can stupefy our reason and fortify our faith in mankind.

11

HUMANISM VERSUS NATURALISM

For Jacques Monod, one of the founders of molecular biology, life is a fluke which cannot be deduced from the nature of things, but once it has emerged, it evolves by the natural selection of random mutations. The human species is no different from any other in being a lucky throw in the cosmic lottery.

This is a hard truth for us to accept. As Monod writes, 'The liberal societies of the West still pay lip-service to, and present as a basis for morality, a disgusting farrago of Judeo-Christian religiosity, scientistic progressism, belief in the "natural" rights of man and utilitarian pragmatism.' Man must set these errors aside and accept that his/her existence is entirely accidental. He 'must at last awake out of his millenary dream and discover his total solitude, his fundamental isolation. He must realise that, like a gypsy, he lives on the boundary of an alien world; a world that is deaf to his music and as indifferent to his hopes as it is to his suffering and his crimes'.

Monod is right that it is hard to accept the fact that humans are no different from other animals. He does not accept it himself. He rightly scorns the modern worldview, but his own philosophy is another version of the same sordid mishmash. For Monod, humanity is a uniquely privileged species. It alone knows that its existence is an accident, and it alone can take charge of its destiny. Like the Christians, Monod believes humankind finds itself in an alien world, and insists that it must make a choice between good and evil: 'The kingdom above or the darkness below: it is for him to choose.' In this fantasy, mankind in the future will be different not only from any other animal but also from anything it has ever been. The Christians who resisted Darwin's theory feared that it left humanity looking insignificant. They need not have worried. Darwinism has been used to put humankind back on its pedestal.

Like many others, Monod runs together two irreconcilable philosophies – humanism and naturalism. Darwin's theory shows the truth of naturalism: we are animals like any other; our fate and that of the rest of life on Earth are the same. Yet, in an irony all the more exquisite because no one has noticed it, Darwinism is now the central prop of the humanist faith that we can transcend our animal natures and rule the Earth.

12

STRAW DOGS

Humanism is a secular religion thrown together from decaying scraps of Christian myth. In contrast, the Gaia hypothesis – the theory that the Earth is a self-regulating system whose behaviour resembles in some ways that of an organism – embodies the most rigorous scientific naturalism.

In James Lovelock's model of Daisyworld, a planet containing only black and white daisies becomes one in which global temperature is self-regulating. Daisyworld is lit by a sun that grows hotter over time. White daisies reflect the sun's heat, thereby cooling the surface of the planet, while black daisies absorb the heat, so warming the surface. Without any element of purpose, these daisies interact to cool their world despite the warming sun.

All that is required to bring a self-regulating biosphere into existence are mechanistic and stochastic processes, which can be modelled in a computer simulation. Joel de Rosnay explains:

> The simulation . . . starts with a low temperature. The black daisies, which absorb the heat of the sun better, survive, develop and occupy a large area. As a result, the temperature of the soil increases, becoming more favourable to life. The black daisies reproduce at a high rate but cover too much area, and temperature increases above a critical point; the black daisies die off en masse. But the white ones adapt, develop, and colonize large areas, reflecting the heat and cooling the planet again. The temperature drops – too much. The white daisies die and the black ones return in profusion. After a certain number of fluctuations, a 'mosaic' of black and white areas begins to coexist and coevolve on the

planet's surface. Individual daisies are born and die, but the two populations, through successive heating and cooling, maintain an average temperature favourable to the life of both species, and this temperature fluctuates around an optimal balance. No one set the temperature, it simply emerged – the result of the daisies' behaviour and their co-evolution.

Daisyworld arises from chance and necessity.

As the Daisyworld model shows, the Gaia hypothesis is consistent with the narrowest scientific orthodoxy. Even so, the hostility of scientific fundamentalists to it is well founded. At bottom the conflict between Gaia theory and current orthodoxy is not a scientific controversy. It is a collision of myths – one formed by Christianity, the other by a much older faith.

Gaia theory re-establishes the link between humans and the rest of nature which was affirmed in mankind's primordial religion, animism. In monotheistic faiths God is the final guarantee of meaning in human life. For Gaia, human life has no more meaning than the life of slime mould.

Lovelock has written that Gaia was named after the ancient Greek goddess of the Earth at the suggestion of his friend the novelist William Golding. But the idea of Gaia is anticipated most clearly in a line from the *Tao Te Ching*, the oldest Taoist scripture. In ancient Chinese rituals, straw dogs were used as offerings to the gods. During the ritual they were treated with the utmost reverence. When it was over and they were no longer needed they were trampled on and tossed aside: 'Heaven and earth are ruthless, and treat the myriad creatures as straw dogs.' If humans disturb the balance of the Earth they will be trampled on and tossed aside. Critics of Gaia theory say they reject it because it is unscientific. The truth is that they fear and hate it because it means that humans can never be other than straw dogs.

2
THE DECEPTION

How far is truth susceptible of embodiment? – that is
the question, that is the experiment.

NIETZSCHE

1

AT THE MASKED BALL

'I should liken Kant to a man at a ball, who all evening has been carrying on a love affair with a masked beauty in the vain hope of making a conquest, when at last she throws off her mask and reveals herself to be his wife.' In Schopenhauer's fable the wife masquerading as an unknown beauty was Christianity. Today it is humanism.

What Schopenhauer wrote of Kant is no less true today. As commonly practised, philosophy is the attempt to find good reasons for conventional beliefs. In Kant's time the creed of conventional people was Christian, now it is humanist. Nor are these two faiths so different from one another. Over the past two hundred years, philosophy has shaken off Christian faith. It has not given up Christianity's cardinal error – the belief that humans are radically different from all other animals.

Philosophy has been a masked ball in which a religious image of humankind is renewed in the guise of humanist ideas of progress and enlightenment. Even philosophy's greatest unmaskers have ended up as figures in the masquerade. Removing the masks from our animal faces is a task that has hardly begun.

Other animals are born, seek mates, forage for food and die. That is all. But we humans – we think – are different. We are *persons*, whose actions are the results of their *choices*. Other animals pass their lives unawares, but we are *conscious*. Our image of ourselves is formed from our ingrained belief that *consciousness, selfhood* and *free will* are what define us as human beings, and raise us above all other creatures.

In our more detached moments, we admit that this view of ourselves is flawed. Our lives are more like fragmentary dreams than the enactments of conscious selves. We control very little of what we most care about; many of our most fateful decisions are made unbeknownst to ourselves. Yet we insist that *mankind* can achieve what *we* cannot: conscious mastery of its existence. This is the creed of those who have given up an irrational belief in God for an irrational faith in mankind. But what if we give up the empty hopes of Christianity and humanism? Once we switch off the sound-track – the babble of God and immortality, progress and humanity – what sense can we make of our lives?

2

SCHOPENHAUER'S CRUX

The first and still unsurpassed critique of humanism was made by Arthur Schopenhauer. This combative bachelor, who retired to Frankfurt in 1833 for the last decades of his reclusive life because he thought the city had 'no floods', 'better cafés', 'a skilful dentist and less bad physicians', brought the way we think about ourselves to a crux we have yet to resolve.

A hundred years ago, Schopenhauer was vastly influential. Writers including Thomas Hardy and Joseph Conrad, Leo Tolstoy and Thomas Mann, were deeply affected by his philosophy, and the works of musicians and painters such as Schoenberg and de Chirico were infused with his ideas. If he is scarcely read today, it is because few great modern thinkers have gone so much against the spirit of their time and ours.

Schopenhauer scorned the ideas of universal emancipation that had begun to spread through Europe in the mid-nineteenth century. In political terms, he was a reactionary liberal, looking to the state only to protect his life and property. He viewed the revolutionary movements of his day with a mixture of horror and contempt, offering his opera glasses for use as a telescopic rifle sight to guardsmen firing on a crowd during the popular demonstrations of 1848. Yet he also scorned the official philosophy of the day, viewing Hegel – Europe's most widely esteemed philosopher and a massive influence on later thinkers such as Marx – as little more than an apologist for state power.

In his personal life, Schopenhauer was guarded and self-possessed. He had an acute sense of the dangers of human life. He slept with loaded pistols by his bed and refused to allow his barber to shave his neck. He delighted in company but often preferred his own. He never married but seems to have been sexually highly active. An erotic diary found in his

papers at his death was burnt by his executor, but his celebrated essay 'On Women' gave him a reputation for mi-
sogyny that has stayed with him ever since.

He had a love of habit. During his later life in Frankfurt
he followed an unvarying daily routine. Getting up around
seven, he would write until noon, play the flute for half an
hour, then go out to lunch, always in the same place.
Afterwards he returned to his rooms, read until four, then
went for a two-hour walk, ending up at a library where he
read the London *Times*. In the evening he went to a play or a
concert, after which he had a light supper in a hotel called the
Englischer Hof. He kept to this regime for nearly thirty years.

One of the few memorable episodes in Schopenhauer's
uneventful life came about as a result of his hatred of noise.
Infuriated by a seamstress talking outside his rooms, Schopenhauer pushed her down a flight of stairs. The woman
was injured and sued him. He lost the case, and as a result
had to give her a quarterly sum of money for the rest of her
life. When she died, he wrote in Latin on her death certifi-
cate: 'Obit anus, abit onus' (the old woman dies, the burden
departs). A disbeliever in the reality of the self, Schopenhauer devoted his life to himself.

Yet it is not Schopenhauer's life or personality that account
for his neglect. It is his philosophy, which – so far as Europe
is concerned, anyhow – is more subversive of humanist hopes
than any other.

Schopenhauer believed that philosophy was ruled by
Christian prejudices. He devoted much of his life to dissect-
ing the influence of these prejudices on Immanuel Kant, a

thinker he admired more than any other, but whose philosophy he attacked relentlessly as a secular version of Christianity. Kant's philosophy was one of the main strands in the Enlightenment – the movement of progressive thinkers that sprang up throughout much of Europe in the eighteenth century. The thinkers of the Enlightenment aimed to replace traditional religion by faith in humanity. But the upshot of Schopenhauer's criticism of Kant is that the Enlightenment was only a secular version of Christianity's central mistake.

For Christians, humans are created by God and possess free will, for humanists they are self-determining beings. Either way, they are quite different from all other animals. In contrast, for Schopenhauer we are at one with other animals in our innermost essence. We think we are separated from other humans and even more from other animals by the fact that we are distinct individuals. But that individuality is an illusion. Like other animals, we are embodiments of universal Will, the struggling, suffering energy that animates everything in the world.

Schopenhauer was the first major European thinker to know anything about Indian philosophy, and he remains the only one to have absorbed and accepted its central doctrine – that the free, conscious individual who is the core of Christianity and humanism is an error that conceals from us what we really are. But it was a view he had arrived at independently, through his devastating criticism of Kant.

Kant wrote that David Hume aroused him from dogmatic slumber. He was certainly shaken by the great eighteenth-century Scottish philosopher's profound scepticism. Traditional metaphysicians claimed to demonstrate the existence of God, the freedom of the will and the immortality of the soul. In Hume's view, we cannot even know that the external world really exists. Indeed we do not even know that we ourselves exist, since all we find when we look within is a bundle of sensations. Hume concluded that, knowing nothing, we must follow the ancient Greek Sceptics, and rely on nature and habit to guide our lives.

Kant's dogmatic slumber may have been disturbed by Hume's scepticism, but it was not long before he was snoring soundly again. Kant accepted Hume's argument that we cannot know things in themselves, only the phenomena that are given us in experience. The reality lying behind experience – what Kant called the noumenal world of things in themselves – is unknowable. But he refused to accept Hume's sceptical conclusion. According to Kant, I could not have the experience of choosing freely if I were only the empirical organism I seem to be. It is only because I belong in the noumenal world outside space and time that I can live my life according to moral principles.

Like most philosophers, Kant worked to shore up the conventional beliefs of his time. Schopenhauer did the opposite. Accepting the arguments of Hume and Kant that the world is unknowable, he concluded that both the world and the individual subject that imagines it knows it are *maya*, dreamlike constructions with no basis in reality. Morality is not a set of laws or principles. It is a feeling – the feeling of compassion for the suffering of others which is made possible by the fact that separate individuals are finally figments. Here Schopenhauer's thought converges with the Vedanta and

Buddhism, which despite their differences share the central insight that individual selfhood is an illusion.

Schopenhauer accepted the sceptical side of Kant's philosophy and turned it against him. Kant demonstrated that we are trapped in the world of phenomena and cannot know things in themselves. Schopenhauer went one step further and observed that we ourselves belong in the world of appearances.

Unlike Kant, Schopenhauer was ready to follow his thoughts wherever they led. Kant argued that unless we accept that we are autonomous, freely choosing selves we cannot make sense of our moral experience. Schopenhauer responded that our actual experience is not of freely choosing the way we live but of being driven along by our bodily needs – by fear, hunger and, above all, sex. Sex, as Schopenhauer wrote in one of the many inimitably vivid passages that enliven his works, 'is the ultimate goal of nearly all human effort. . . . It knows how to slip its love notes and ringlets into ministerial portfolios and philosophical manuscripts'. When we are in the grip of sexual love we tell ourselves we will be happy once it is satisfied; but this is only a mirage. Sexual passion enables the species to reproduce; it cares nothing for individual well-being or personal autonomy. It is not true that our experience compels us to think of ourselves as free agents. On the contrary, if we look at ourselves truthfully we know we are not.

Schopenhauer believed he had the definitive answer to the metaphysical questions that had plagued thinkers since philosophy began. Using his critique of Kant to batter down the ordinary view of time, space and cause and effect, he offered a different vision of the world – one in which there are no separate things at all, in which plurality and difference do not exist, and there is only the ceaseless striving he calls Will.

This is an arresting picture, but we need not take it as the ultimate truth about the nature of things. Instead we may take it as a metaphor for a truth about ourselves. We like to think reason guides our lives, but reason itself is only – as Schopenhauer puts it, echoing Hume – the hard-pressed servant of the will. Our intellects are not impartial observers of the world but active participants in it. They shape a view of it that helps us in our struggles. Among the imaginary constructions created by the intellect working in the service of the will, perhaps the most delusive is the view it gives us of ourselves – as continuing, unified individuals.

Kant tried to protect our most cherished notions – above all our ideas of personal identity, free will and moral autonomy – from the solvent of sceptical doubt. Putting them to the acid test of actual experience, Schopenhauer showed that they melt way. In doing so he destroyed Kant's philosophy, and with it the idea of the human subject that underpins both Christianity and humanism.

3

NIETZSCHE'S 'OPTIMISM'

Schopenhauer wrote: 'What history relates is in fact only the long, heavy and confused dream of mankind.' Nietzsche attacked Schopenhauer's view of history as pessimism. Yet in denying that history has any meaning, Schopenhauer was simply drawing the last consequence of what Nietzsche was later to call 'the death of God'.

Nietzsche was an inveterately religious thinker, whose incessant attacks on Christian beliefs and values attest to the fact that he could never shake them off. The incomparable atheist and indefatigable scourge of Christian values came from a line of clergymen. Born in 1844, he was the son of a Lutheran minister, and both his father and his mother were themselves children of ministers. Appointed to the chair of classical languages at Basle University when he was only twenty-four, ill health forced Nietzsche to give up his precociously brilliant academic career. For the rest of his life he led a wandering, ascetic existence. Criss-crossing Europe in search of good weather and peace of mind, he lived in small guesthouses, where his solitary ways and gentle manners earned him the tag 'the little saint'. Despite a tangled and inconclusive involvement with a remarkable woman, Lou Andreas-Salome, he never had a lover and very likely hardly any sex life, yet somehow he seems to have contracted syphilis. It was probably the progressive effect of the disease on the brain that triggered his mental breakdown in Turin in January 1889, when he embraced a horse that he saw being flogged by a coachman on the Piazza Carlo Alberto. After that, his mind gone, he lingered in a half-world of physical and mental paralysis until he died in 1900.

Nietzsche's collapse was prefigured in his thought. He had dreamt of such an incident the previous May, and written about the dream in a letter. Possibly, Nietzsche's gesture mimicked that of Raskolnikov, the criminal hero of a novel Nietzsche had read and much admired, Dostoevsky's *Crime and Punishment*, who dreamt of throwing his arms around a mistreated horse. Or perhaps it can be seen as an attempt to beg forgiveness from the animal for the cruel treatment it had received, a cruelty that Nietzsche may well have believed flowed from the errors of philosophers such as Descartes, who held that animals were unfeeling machines.

It is ironic that Nietzsche's breakdown should have been triggered by the sight of an animal being cruelly treated. Against Schopenhauer, Nietzsche had often argued that the best people should cultivate a taste for cruelty. Schopenhauer had been Nietzsche's first love in philosophy, but in his early book *The Birth of Tragedy*, Nietzsche is already urging that pity – the supreme virtue according to Schopenhauer – should not be allowed to destroy the joy of life. In later writings, Nietzsche insisted that pity was not the supreme virtue but rather a sign of weak vitality. If pity became the core of ethics, the result would only be more suffering, as misery became contagious and happiness an object of suspicion. Schopenhauer argued that we achieve compassion for other living things by 'turning away from the Will' – by ceasing to care about our own well-being and survival. In Nietzsche's view, this morality of compassion was anti-life. Life was indeed cruel; but it was better to glorify the Will than deny it. In *The Birth of Tragedy*, Nietzsche returned to the ancient Greek cult of the god Dionysus, 'the wild spirit of antithesis and paradox, of immediate presence and complete remoteness, of bliss and horror, of infinite vitality and the cruelest destruction', whose death and rebirth were celebrated to mark the renewal of life after winter. This was Nietzsche's answer to Schopenhauer's 'pessimism' – a 'Dionysian' affirmation of life in all its cruelty. Yet it was not the coldly cheerful Schopenhauer – 'the flute-playing pessimist', as Nietzsche scornfully described him – who was destroyed by pity. It was Nietzsche, whose acute sensitivity to the pain of the world tormented him throughout his life. In his last days of sanity, he sent euphoric letters to friends, alternately signed 'Dionysus' and 'The Crucified'.

The circumstances of Nietzsche's breakdown suggest another irony. Unlike Nietzsche, Schopenhauer turned away from Christianity and never looked back, and one of the core Christian beliefs that he left behind was a belief in the significance of human history. For Christians, it is because they occur in history that the lives of humans have a meaning that the lives of other animals do not. What enables humans to have a history is that – unlike other animals – they can freely choose how to live their lives. They are given this freedom by God, who created them in his own image.

If we truly leave Christianity behind, we must give up the idea that human history has a meaning. Neither in the ancient pagan world nor in any other culture has human history ever been thought to have an overarching significance. In Greece and Rome, it was a series of natural cycles of growth and decline. In India, it was a collective dream, endlessly repeated. The idea that history must make sense is just a Christian prejudice.

If you believe that humans are animals, there can be no such thing as the history of humanity, only the lives of particular humans. If we speak of the history of the species at all, it is only to signify the unknowable sum of these lives. As with other animals, some lives are happy, others wretched. None has a meaning that lies beyond itself.

Looking for meaning in history is like looking for patterns in clouds. Nietzsche knew this; but he could not accept it. He was trapped in the chalk circle of Christian hopes. A believer to the end, he never gave up the absurd faith that something could be made of the human animal. He invented the ridiculous figure of the Superman to give history meaning it had not had before. He hoped that humankind would thereby be awakened from its long sleep. As could have been foreseen, he succeeded only in adding further nightmares to its confused dream.

4

HEIDEGGER'S HUMANISM

Heidegger tells us that, by comparison with man, animals are 'world-poor'. Animals merely exist, reacting to the things they encounter around them; whereas humans are makers of the worlds they inhabit. Why does Heidegger believe this? Because he cannot rid himself of the prejudice that humans are necessary in the scheme of things, whereas other animals are not.

In his *Letter on Humanism*, Heidegger claims to reject the man-centred thinking that has prevailed – ever since the pre-Socratics, he tells us – in Western philosophy. In the past, philosophers were concerned only with the human, now they should put the human on one side and concern themselves with 'Being'. But Heidegger turns to 'Being' for the same reason that Christians turn to God – to affirm the unique place of humans in the world.

Like Nietzsche, Heidegger was a postmonotheist – an unbeliever who could not give up Christian hopes. In his great first book, *Being and Time*, he sets out a view of human existence that is supposed to depend at no point on religion. Yet every one of the categories of thought he deploys – 'thrownness' (*Dasein*), 'uncanniness' (*Unheimlichkeit*), 'guilt' (*Schuld*) – is a secular version of a Christian idea. We are 'thrown' into the world, which remains always foreign or 'uncanny' to us, and in which we can never be truly at home. Again, whatever we do, we cannot escape guilt; we are condemned to choose without having any ground for our choices, which will always be somehow mysteriously at fault. Obviously, these are the Christian ideas of the Fall of Man and Original Sin, recycled by Heidegger with an existential-sounding twist.

In his later writings, Heidegger declared that he had abandoned humanism in order to concern himself with 'Being'. In fact, since he sought in Being what Christians believe they find in God, he no more gave up humanism than Nietzsche did. Admittedly he is never clear what Being signifies. Often he writes as if it is altogether indefinable. But whatever Being may be, there can be no doubt that for Heidegger it gives humans a unique standing in the world.

For Heidegger, humans are the site in which Being is disclosed. Without humans, Being would be silent. Meister Eckardt and Angelus Silesius, German mystics whose writings Heidegger seems to have studied closely, said much the same: God needs man as much as man needs God. For these mystics, humans stand at the centre of the world, everything else is marginal. Other animals are deaf-mutes; only through humans can God speak and be heard.

Heidegger sees everything that lives solely from the standpoint of its relations with humans. The differences between living creatures count for nothing in comparison with their difference from humans. Molluscs and mice are the same as bats and gorillas, badgers and wolves are no different from crabs and gnats. All are 'world-poor', none has the power to 'disclose Being'. This is only the old anthropocentric conceit, rendered anew in the idiom of a secular Gnostic.

Heidegger praised 'the crooked path of thought', but he did so because he believed it led back to 'home'. In Heidegger's never-renounced engagement with Nazism, the quest for 'home' became a hatred of hybrid thinking and the worship of a deadly unity of will. There can be little doubt that Heidegger's flirtation with Nazism was in part an exercise in opportunism. In May 1933, with the help of Nazi officials, he was appointed Rector of the University of Freiburg. He used the post to give speeches in support of Hitler's policies, including one in November 1933 in which he pronounced, 'The Fuhrer himself and alone is the present and future German reality and its law.' At the same time he broke off relations with students and colleagues (such as his old friend and former teacher Edmund Husserl) who were Jewish. In acting in this way, Heidegger was not much different from many other German academics at the time.

But Heidegger's involvement with Nazism went deeper than cowardice and power worship. It expressed an impulse integral to his thinking. By contrast with Nietzsche, a nomad who wrote for travellers like himself and who was able to put so much in question because he belonged nowhere, Heidegger always yearned desperately to belong. For him, thinking was not an adventure whose charm comes from the fact that one cannot know where it leads. It was a long detour, at the end of which lay the peace that comes from no longer having to think. In his rectorial address at Freiburg, Heidegger came close to saying as much, leading the observer Karl Lowith to comment that it was not quite clear whether one should now study the pre-Socratic philosophers or join the Brownshirts.

Heidegger claimed that in his later thought he turned away from humanism. Yet, except perhaps in his last years, he showed no interest in traditions in which the human subject is not central. He held resolutely to the European tradition because he believed that in it alone 'the question of Being' had been rightly posed. It was this belief that led him to assert that Greek and German are the only truly 'philosophical' languages – as if the subtle reasonings of Nagarjuna, Chuang-Tzu and Dogen, Jey Tsong Khapa, Averroës and Maimonides could not be philosophy because Indian,

Chinese, Japanese, Tibetan, Arab and Jewish thinkers did not write in these European tongues. Purged of alien voices and returned to its primordial purity, philosophy could once again become the voice of Being. Philosophers could read the runes of history, and know what mankind was called upon to do – as Heidegger claimed he did in Germany in the thirties. Seldom has a philosopher claimed so much for himself, or been so deluded.

In Heidegger's last writings he speaks of *Gelassenheit*, or releasement – a way of thinking and living that has turned away from willing. Perhaps this reflects the influence on him of East Asian thought, particularly Taoism. More likely, Heidegger's *Gelassenheit* is only the release from willing that Schopenhauer had long before seen as the source of art. In art, and above all in music, we forget the practical interests and strivings that together make up 'the will'. By doing so we forget ourselves, Schopenhauer claimed: we see the world from a standpoint of selfless contemplation. In the last phase of his thought, the only one in which he really turned away from humanism, Heidegger did little more than return to Schopenhauer by a roundabout route.

5

CONVERSING WITH LIONS

'If a lion could talk, we could not understand him,' the philosopher Ludwig Wittgenstein once said. 'It's clear that

Wittgenstein hadn't spent much time with lions,' commented the gambler and conservationist John Aspinall.

Like Heidegger, Wittgenstein was a humanist in a venerable European tradition. Philosophers from Plato to Hegel have interpreted the world as if it was a mirror of human thinking. Later philosophers such as Heidegger and Wittgenstein went further, and claimed that the world is a construction of human thought. In all these philosophies, the world acquires a significance from the fact that humans have appeared in it. In fact, until humans arrive, there is hardly a world at all.

Wittgenstein believed that his later thought had transcended traditional philosophy, but at bottom it is not much more than another version of the oldest of philosophies – Idealism. For idealists, thought is the final reality; there is nothing that is independent of mind. In practice, this means that the world is a human invention. If solipsism is the belief that only I exist, Idealism is the belief that only humans exist.

Unusual, possibly unique amongst philosophers in producing two different and opposed systems of thought, Wittgenstein tried in his first philosophy to give an account of thought and language in which it mirrored the logical structure of the world. This is the philosophy of his *Tractatus Logico-Philosophicus*. By the time he had formulated his second philosophy, most clearly expressed in his *Philosophical Investigations*, Wittgenstein had given up the idea that language could mirror the world. Instead he denied that any sense could be given to the idea of a world existing apart from language. This led him to give up his earlier mystical belief, expressed in the *Tractatus* and owing a good deal to Schopenhauer, that there are some things that cannot be expressed in words and about which we must be silent – in Wittgenstein's later philosophy, there is nothing that cannot be said. Despite the power and subtlety with which Wittgenstein developed this view, it is only Idealism stated in linguistic terms.

Wittgenstein took it as given that we cannot talk to lions. If humans were found among whom conversation with other animals was normal, he could say only that we – that's to say, he – could not understand them. He wrote: 'The common behaviour of mankind is the system of reference by means of which we interpret an unknown language.' We might more truly say: The common behaviour of animals is the system of reference by means of which we interpret the brute noises of humans.

6

'POSTMODERNISM'

Postmodernists tell us there is no such thing as nature, only the floating world of our own constructions. All talk of human nature is spurned as dogmatic and reactionary. Let us put these phoney absolutes aside, say the postmodernists, and accept that the world is what we make of it.

Postmodernists parade their relativism as a superior kind of humility – the modest acceptance that we cannot claim to have the truth. In fact, the postmodern denial of truth is the worst kind of arrogance. In denying that the natural world exists independently of our beliefs about it, postmodernists are implicitly rejecting any limit on human ambitions. By making human beliefs the final arbiter of reality, they are effectively claiming that nothing exists unless it appears in human consciousness.

The idea that there is no such thing as truth may be fashionable, but it is hardly new. Two and half thousand years ago, Protagoras, the first of the Greek sophists, declared, 'Man is the measure of all things.' He meant human individuals, not the species; but the implication is the same. Humans decide what is real and what is not. Postmodernism is just the latest fad in anthropocentrism.

7

ANIMAL FAITH

Philosophers have always tried to show that we are not like other animals, sniffing their way uncertainly through the world. Yet after all the work of Plato and Spinoza, Descartes and Bertrand Russell, we have no more reason than other animals do for believing that the sun will rise tomorrow.

8

PLATO AND THE ALPHABET

The calls of birds and the traces left by wolves to mark off their territories are no less forms of language than the songs of humans. What is distinctively human is not the capacity for language. It is the crystallisation of language in writing.

From its humble beginnings as a means of stocktaking and tallying debts, writing gave humans the power to preserve their thoughts and experiences from time. In oral cultures this was attempted by feats of memory, but with the invention of writing human experience could be preserved when no memory of it remained. The *Iliad* must have been handed down as a song for many generations, but without writing we would not have the vision of an archaic world it preserves for us today.

Writing creates an artificial memory, whereby humans can enlarge their experience beyond the limits of one generation or one way of life. At the same time it has allowed them to invent a world of abstract entities and mistake them for reality. The development of writing has enabled them to construct philosophies in which they no longer belong in the natural world.

The earliest forms of writing preserved many links with the natural world. The pictographs of Sumer were metaphors of sensuous realities. With the evolution of phonetic writing those links were severed. Writing no longer pointed outwards to a world humans shared with other animals. Henceforth its signs pointed backwards to the human mouth, which soon became the source of all sense.

When twentieth-century philosophers such as Fritz Mauthner and Wittgenstein attacked the superstitious reverence for words they found in philosophers such as Plato they were criticising a by-product of phonetic writing. It is scarcely possible to imagine a philosophy such as Platonism emerging in an oral culture. It is equally difficult to imagine it in Sumeria. How could a world of bodiless Forms be represented in pictograms? How could abstract entities be represented as the ultimate realities in a mode of writing that still recalled the realm of the senses?

It is significant that nothing resembling Platonism arose in China. Classical Chinese script is not ideographic, as used to be thought; but because of what A. C. Graham terms its 'combination of graphic wealth with phonetic poverty' it did not encourage the kind of abstract thinking that produced Plato's philosophy. Plato was what historians of philosophy call a realist – he believed that abstract terms designated spiritual or intellectual entities. In contrast, throughout its long history, Chinese thought has been nominalist – it has understood that even the most abstract terms are only labels, names for the diversity of things in the world. As a result, Chinese thinkers have rarely mistaken ideas for facts.

Plato's legacy to European thought was a trio of capital letters – the Good, the Beautiful and the True. Wars have been fought and tyrannies established, cultures have been ravaged and peoples exterminated, in the service of these abstractions. Europe owes much of its murderous history to errors of thinking engendered by the alphabet.

9

AGAINST THE CULT OF PERSONALITY

If humanists are to be believed, the Earth – with its vast wealth of ecosystems and life forms – had no value until humans came onto the scene. Value is only a shadow cast by humans desiring or choosing. Only *persons* have any kind of intrinsic worth. Among Christians the cult of personhood may be forgiven. For them, everything of value in the world emanates from a divine person, in whose image humans are made. But once we have relinquished Christianity the very idea of the person becomes suspect.

A person is someone who believes that she authors her own life through her choices. That is not the way most humans have ever lived. Nor is it how many of those with the best lives have seen themselves. Did the protagonists in the *Odyssey* or the *Bhagavad-Gita* think of themselves as persons? Did the characters in *The Canterbury Tales*? Are we to believe that bushido warriors in Edo Japan, princes and minstrels in medieval Europe, Renaissance courtesans and Mongol nomads were lacking because their lives failed to square with a modern ideal of personal autonomy?

Being a person is not the essence of humanity, only – as the word's history suggests – one of its masks. Persons are only humans who have donned the mask that has been handed down in Europe over the past few generations, and taken it for their face.

10

THE POVERTY OF CONSCIOUSNESS

Consciousness counts for less in the scheme of things than we have been taught. Plato identified ultimate reality with what was perceived by humans in their most conscious moments; and it has been an axiom since Descartes that knowledge presupposes conscious awareness. But sensation and perception do not depend on consciousness, still less on self-awareness. They exist throughout the animal and plant kingdoms.

The senses of plants 'are sophisticated; some can detect the lightest touch (better than the activity of human fingertips), and they all have a sense of vision'. The oldest and simplest microbial life forms have senses that resemble those of humans. Halobacteria date back to the beginnings of life on earth. They are organisms which can detect and respond to light by virtue of a compound called rhodopsin – the same compound, present as a pigment in human eyes, that enables us to see. We look at the world through eyes of ancient mud.

The old dualisms tell us that matter lacks intelligence and knowledge can exist only where there are minds. In truth, knowledge does not need minds, or even nervous systems. It is found in all living things. As Margulis has written:

Small mammals communicate the coming earth-quake or cloudburst. Trees release 'volatiles', substances that warn their neighbours that gypsy moth larvae are attacking their leaves ... extinct packs of wolves and flocks of dinosaurs enjoyed their own proprioceptive social communication. ... Gaia, the physiologically regulated Earth, enjoyed proprioceptive global communication long before people evolved.

Bacteria act on knowledge of their environment: sensing chemical differences, they swim towards sugar and away from acid. The immune systems of more complicated organisms display learning and memory. 'Living systems are cognitive systems. And living as a process is a process of cognition. This statement is valid for all organisms, with or without a nervous system.'

Even in living things in which awareness is highly developed, perception and thought normally go on without consciousness. Nowhere is this more true than in humans. Conscious perception is only a fraction of what we know through our senses. By far the greater part we receive through subliminal perception. What surfaces in consciousness are fading shadows of things we know already.

Consciousness is a variable, not a constant, and its fluctuations are indispensable to our survival. We fall into sleep in obedience to a primordial circadian rhythm; we nightly inhabit the virtual worlds of dreams; nearly all our daily doings go on without conscious awareness; our deepest motivations are shut away from conscious scrutiny; nearly all of our mental life takes place unknown to us; the most creative acts in the life of the mind come to pass unawares. Very little that is of consequence in our lives requires consciousness. Much that is vitally important comes about only in its absence.

Plato and Descartes tell us that consciousness is what marks off humans from other animals. Plato believed that ultimate reality is spiritual, and that humans are alone among animals in being at least dimly conscious of it. Descartes saw humans as thinking beings. He declared he knew he existed only because he found himself thinking – 'Cogito, ergo sum' (I think, therefore I am) – and that animals were mere machines. Yet cats, dogs and horses display awareness of their surroundings; they experience themselves as acting or failing to act; they have thoughts and sensations. As primatologists have shown, our nearest evolutionary kin among the apes have many of the mental capacities we are accustomed to think belong only to ourselves. Despite an ancient tradition that tells us otherwise, there is nothing uniquely human in conscious awareness.

Where other animals differ from humans is in lacking the sensation of selfhood. In this they are not altogether unfortunate. Self-awareness is as much a disability as a power. The most accomplished pianist is not the one who is most aware of her movements when she plays. The best craftsman may not know how he works. Very often we are at our most skilful when we are least self-aware. That may be why many cultures have sought to disrupt or diminish self-conscious awareness. In Japan, archers are taught that they will hit the target only when they no longer think of it – or themselves.

The meditative states that have long been cultivated in Eastern traditions are often described as techniques for heightening consciousness. In fact they are ways of bypassing it. Drugs, fasting, divination and dance are only the most familiar examples. In earlier times, architecture was used to produce a systematic derangement of the senses. As Rebecca Stone Miller wrote of ancient Andean art: 'Chavin is a very complex, "baroque" and esoteric style, intentionally difficult to decipher, intended to disorient, and ultimately to transport the viewer into alternative realities.' Among modern architects, Gaudí is one of the few who sought to alter everyday perception. But some of the most successful experiments in twentieth-century painting were attempts to do just that. The Surrealists understood that if we are to look at the world afresh we must recover the vision of things we are given by unconscious or subliminal perception. Artists such as Giorgio de Chirico and Max Ernst did not give up representing things as we ordinarily see them because they were captivated by novel techniques. They experimented with new techniques so as to recover a vision of things that may once have been common. In the earliest art there are traces of what the senses showed before they were overlaid by conscious awareness. The artists of the Upper Paleolithic 'had no history,' N. K. Sandars observes. 'This does not mean that their minds were an intellectual void, a tabula rasa waiting to be filled with the experiences of civilisation. The mind of the artist was already stored with the million years of his life as a reflective being. Most of this is now beyond our reach.'

Subliminal perception – perception that occurs without conscious awareness – is not an anomaly but the norm. Most of what we perceive of the world comes not from conscious observation but from a continuous process of unconscious scanning: 'Unconscious vision . . . [has] proved to be capable of . . . gathering more information than a conscious scrutiny lasting a hundred times longer . . . the undifferentiated structure of unconscious vision . . . displays scanning powers that are superior to conscious vision.' These words were written by the psychoanalyst Anton Ehrenzweig in the course of developing a theory of art, but the sciences tell the same story. The early-twentieth-century neurologist O. Potzl showed that images shown to waking people too briefly to be noticed or consciously remembered surface in their dreams. Again, in the phenomenon of blindsight, brain-damaged people can describe and manipulate objects that fall outside their field of vision.

These examples come from scientific research into anomalous experiences, but subliminal perception is not something that occurs on the margins of our lives. It is continuous and all-pervasive. It was in order to exploit this fact that enterprises such as the Subliminal Projection Company were formed to influence consumer behaviour by the use of messages too brief to be registered in conscious awareness. Subliminal advertising works – which is why in most countries it was effectively banned around forty years ago.

The world we see through the filter of conscious awareness is a fragment of that which is given us by subliminal vision.

Our senses have been censored so that our lives can flow more easily. Yet we rely on our preconscious view of the world in everything we do. To equate what we know with what we learn though conscious awareness is a cardinal error. The life of the mind is like that of the body. If it depended on conscious awareness or control it would fail entirely.

11

LORD JIM'S JUMP

In his novel *Lord Jim*, Joseph Conrad writes of the son of an English parson who is charmed by the heroic vision of life as a seaman. He takes up the seafaring life only to be disillusioned: 'entering the regions so well known to his imagination, [he] found them strangely barren of adventure'. Yet he does not go back, but goes on with his life at sea. In his mid-twenties, he enlists as first mate on the *Patna*, a battered old steamer. En route to Mecca with a human cargo of eight hundred pilgrims, the *Patna* hits a submerged obstacle and seems about to sink. Leaving the pilgrims to their fate, the ship's German captain and European officers take to a lifeboat they have lowered alongside. At first Jim does nothing, viewing the event almost as a spectator; but finally he jumps, and finds himself in the lifeboat:

'I had jumped.' He checked himself, averted his gaze . . . 'It seems,' he added.

As it turns out, the *Patna* is unharmed, and its Muslim passengers are safely towed to harbour. But Jim's life is changed for ever. The ship's captain disappears, and Jim has to face the disgrace of a public inquiry alone. In private, he is haunted by the feeling that he has betrayed the seaman's ethic of bravery and service. In the years that follow, he seeks anonymity in perpetual travel. He ends up in Patusan, a remote settlement in northwest Sumatra, where he finds sanctuary from the world and becomes Tuan Jim – Lord Jim – the ruler who brings peace to the native people. But events – and his own character – conspire against him. Patusan is invaded by a malign buccaneer, Gentleman Brown, and his gang. Jim arranges for Brown to leave the island, but the pirate murders Jim's friend, the son of the elderly native chieftain. Jim has pledged his life to the safety of the inhabitants of Patusan. He honours the pledge by going to the grieving chieftain, who shoots him dead.

Lord Jim's life is overshadowed by a question he cannot answer. Did he jump? Or was he pushed by events? The idea that we are authors of our actions is required by 'morality'. If Jim is to be held accountable for his jump, he must have been able to act otherwise than he did. That is what free will means – if it means anything. Did Jim do what he did freely? How can he – or anyone else – ever know?

There are many reasons for rejecting the idea of free will, some of them decisive. If our actions are caused then we cannot act otherwise than we do. In that case we cannot be responsible for them. We can be free agents only if we are authors of our acts; but we are ourselves products of chance and necessity. We cannot choose to be what we are born. In that case, we cannot be responsible for what we do.

These are strong arguments against free will; but recent scientific research has weakened it even more. In Benjamin Libet's work on 'the half-second delay', it has been shown that the electrical impulse that initiates action occurs half a second *before* we take the conscious decision to act. We think of ourselves as deliberating what to do, then doing it. In fact, in nearly the whole of our lives, our actions are initiated unconsciously: the brain makes us ready for action, *then* we have the experience of acting. As Libet and his colleagues put it:

> . . . the brain evidently 'decides' to initiate, or, at the least, prepare to initiate the act at a time before there is any reportable subjective awareness that such a decision has taken place . . . cerebral initiation even of a spontaneous voluntary act . . . can and usually does begin *unconsciously*.

If we do not act in the way we think we do, the reason is partly to do with the bandwidth of consciousness – its ability to transmit information measured in terms of bits per second. This is much too narrow to be able to register the information we routinely receive and act on. As organisms active in the world, we process perhaps 14 million bits of information per second. The bandwidth of consciousness is around eighteen bits. This means we have conscious access to about a millionth of the information we daily use to survive.

The upshot of neuroscientific research is that we cannot be the authors of our acts. Libet does retain a faint shadow of free will in his notion of the veto – the capacity of consciousness to stall or abort an act that the brain has initiated. The trouble is that we can never know when – or if – we have exercised the veto. Our subjective experience is frequently, perhaps always, ambiguous.

When we are on the point of acting, we cannot predict what we are about to do. Yet when we look back we may see our decision as a step on a path on which we were already bound. We see our thoughts sometimes as events that happen to us, and sometimes as our acts. Our feeling of freedom comes about through switching between these two angles of vision. Free will is a trick of perspective.

Stuck in an incessant oscillation between the perspective of an actor and that of a spectator, Lord Jim is unable to decide what it is he has done. He hopes to dredge from consciousness something that will end his uncertainty. He is in search of his own character. It is a vain search. For, as Schopenhauer – an author much read by Conrad – had written, whatever identity we may possess is only very dimly accessible to conscious awareness:

It is assumed that the identity of the person rests on that of consciousness. If, however, we understand by this merely the conscious recollection of the course of life, then it is not enough. We know, it is true, something more of the course of our life than of a novel we have formerly read, yet very little indeed. The principal events, the interesting scenes, have been impressed on us; for the rest, a thousand events are forgotten for one that has been retained. The older we become, the more does everything pass us by without a trace. . . . It is true that, in consequence of our relation to the external world, we are accustomed to regard the subject of knowing, the knowing I, as our real self. . . . This, however, is the mere function of the brain, and is not our real self. Our true self, the kernel of our inner nature, is that which is to be found behind this, and which really knows nothing but willing and not-willing. . . .

The knowing-I cannot find the acting self for which it seeks. The unalterable character with which Schopenhauer and sometimes Conrad believed all humans are born may not exist; but we cannot help looking within ourselves to account for what we do. All we find are fragments, like memories of a novel we once read.

Lord Jim can never know why he jumped. That is his fate. As a result, he can never start his life afresh, 'with a clean slate'. The last word on Lord Jim's jump must be given to Marlow, the shrewd and sympathetic narrator of the tale, who writes:

As to me, left alone with the solitary candle, I remained singularly unenlightened. I was no longer young enough to behold at every turn the magnificence that besets our insignificant footsteps in good and evil. I smiled to think that, after all, it was yet he, of us two, who had the light. And I felt sad. A clean slate, did he say? As if the initial word of each our destiny were not graven in imperishable characters on the face of a rock.

12

OUR VIRTUAL SELVES

We think our actions express our decisions. But in nearly all of our life, willing decides nothing. We cannot wake up or fall asleep, remember or forget our dreams, summon or banish our thoughts, by deciding to do so.

When we greet someone on the street we just act, and there is no actor standing behind what we do. Our acts are end points in long sequences of unconscious responses. They arise from a structure of habits and skills that is almost infinitely complicated. Most of our life is enacted without conscious awareness. Nor can it be made conscious. No degree of self-awareness can make us self-transparent.

Freud believed that by bringing repressed memories into conscious awareness we can gain greater control of our lives. So long as they remain inaccessible, we may be puzzled by attacks of anxiety, or beset by recurrent slips of the tongue. Retrieving the memories that lie behind such compulsive behaviour may enable us to alter it.

Freud understood that much of the life of the mind goes on in the absence of consciousness. Perhaps he was right that bringing back to conscious awareness those of our thoughts that are unconscious because we have repressed them can enable us to cope with life better. But the preconscious mental activities that lie behind everyday perception and behaviour cannot be retrieved in this way. Unlike the unconscious mind of which Freud speaks, they are what makes conscious awareness possible.

Our conscious selves arise from processes in which conscious awareness plays only a small part. We resist this fact because it seems to deprive us of control of our lives. We think of our actions as the end-results of our thoughts. Yet much the greater part of everyone's life goes on without thinking. The sense of conscious agency may be an artefact of conflicts among our impulses. When we know what to do we are hardly conscious of doing it. That does not mean we are ruled by instinct or habit. It means we spend our lives coping with what comes along.

We deal with the death of a friend in much the same way we step aside to avoid a falling slate. We may be in doubt as to how to show our sadness or comfort others who have been bereaved, but if we succeed in doing so it is not because we have altered our beliefs or improved our reasonings. It is because we have learnt to cope with things more skilfully.

We see ourselves as unitary, conscious subjects, and our lives as the sum of their doings. Recent cognitive science and ancient Buddhist teachings are at one in viewing this ordinary sense of self as illusive. Both view selfhood in humans as a highly complex and fragmentary thing.

Francisco Varela, a cognitive scientist who has noted the convergence of recent scientific inquiry with Buddhist teachings, has formulated the view of the self they have in common:

> Our microworlds and microidentities do not come all stuck together in one solid, centralized, unitary self, but rather arise and subside in a succession of shifting patterns. In Buddhist terminology, this is the doctrine, whose truth can be verified by direct observation, that the self is empty of self-nature, void of any graspable substantiality.

Cognitive science follows Buddhist teachings in viewing the self as a chimera. Our perceptions are fragments, picked out from an unfathomable richness – but there is no one doing the selecting. Our selves are themselves fragmentary:

> Contrary to what seems to be the case from a cursory introspection, cognition does not flow seamlessly from one 'state' to another, but rather consists in a punctuated succession of behavioural patterns that arise and subside in measurable time. This insight of recent neuroscience – and of cognitive science in general – is fundamental, for it relieves us from the tyranny of searching for a centralised, homuncular quality to account for a cognitive agent's normal behaviour.

The notion that our lives are guided by a homunculus – an inner person directing our behaviour – arises from our ability to view ourselves from the outside. We project a self into our actions because by doing so we can account for the way they seem to hang together. The continuities we find are frequently imaginary, but when they are real it is not because anyone put them there. Our behaviour displays a good deal of order, but it does not come about through any inner person ordering it. As R. A. Brooks writes:

Just as there is no central representation there is no central system. Each activity connects perception to action directly. It is only the observer of the creature who imputes a central representation or central control. The creature itself has none: it is a collection of competing behaviours. Out of the local chaos of their interactions there emerges, in the eye of the observer, a coherent pattern of behaviour.

This account of robot behaviour by a contemporary theorist of artificial intelligence applies no less to humans. We are possessed by the notion that there must be a central controller, when in truth there are only the shifting sceneries of perception and behaviour.

Selfhood in humans is not the expression of any essential unity. It is a pattern of organisation, not unlike that found in insect colonies. Around eighty years ago, the South African poet and naturalist Eugene Marais published *The Soul of the White Ant*, a path-breaking study of the life of termites. In it he gave his reasons for thinking that ants have a soul, or psyche, but one that is communal. The soul of the white ant

72

is not the property of any individual insect, but of the entire nest, the termitary. At the time, this was a revolutionary result; but it has been confirmed by later research.

In an illuminating experiment, the removal of highly efficient insect nurses from a colony led them to forage more and nurse less, while in the main colony less efficient nurses nursed more. When the efficient nurses returned to the main colony they returned to their previous activities:

> What is particularly striking about the insect colony is that we readily admit that its separate components are individuals and that it has no centre of localized 'self'. Yet the whole does behave as a unity and as if there were a coordinating agent present at its centre.

What we observe in insect colonies is no different from what we find in ourselves: as Varela puts it, 'a *selfless* (or virtual) self: a coherent global pattern that emerges from the activity of simple local components, which seems to be centrally located, but is nowhere to be found'. In humans, as in insect colonies, perception and action go on as if there were a self that directs them, when in fact none exists.

We labour under an error. We act in the belief that we are all of one piece, but we are able to cope with things only because we are a succession of fragments. We cannot shake off the sense that we are enduring selves, and yet we know we are not.

13

MR NOBODY

Looking back on his life, the British writer and academic Goronwy Rees found only a succession of disjointed episodes. The discovery led him to question the very idea of personal identity. Rees wrote:

> For as long as I can remember it has always surprised and slightly bewildered me that other people should take it so much for granted that they possess what is usually called a character: that is to say, a personality with its own continuous history which can be described as objectively as the life cycle of a plant or an animal. I have never been able to find anything of that sort in myself. . . .

Rees's life was not a novel but a collection of short stories – a bundle of sensations, linked together by the accidents of memory.

Shooting wildcats in Silesia before Hitler came to power; seeing a gunnery officer's incredulity as a flying fragment cut off his leg at the knee during a naval battle in the Second World War; wandering through the ruins of Germany in the aftermath of war and coming across a vast hangar abandoned by the Luftwaffe in which thousands of men, women and children had contrived makeshift homes for themselves from green branches plucked from the nearby fields; recovering in a hospital ward after a near-fatal accident – he recalled these memories as bright vignettes in a waste of forgotten time.

Rees writes that 'at no time in my life have I had that enviable sensation of constituting a continuous personality, of being something which, in the astonishing words of T. H. Green, "is eternal, is self-determined, and which thinks"'. He quotes approvingly the ironic comment of the great Scottish sceptic David Hume, who looked into himself and likewise found no enduring self: 'Setting aside some metaphysicians . . . I may venture to affirm of the rest of mankind that they are nothing but a collection of perceptions which succeed each other with inconceivable rapidity and are in perpetual flux and movement.' For Hume, selfhood is only a rehearsal of continuities. As he wrote:

The mind is a kind of theatre, where several perceptions successively make their appearance; pass, re-pass, glide away, and mingle in an infinite variety of postures and situations. There is properly no *simplicity* in it at one time, nor *identity* in different; whatever natural propensity we have to imagine that simplicity and identity. The comparison of the theatre must not mislead us. They are the successive perceptions only, that constitute the mind; nor have we the most distant notion of the place, where these scenes are represented, or of the materials, of which this is compos'd.

Hume's experience of finding no simplicity or identity in himself was also Rees's. In a fascinating memoir, Rees's daughter confirms his account of himself as 'Mr Nobody, a man without qualities, a person without a sense of "self"'. Rees's experience may have been unusual in its intensity, as the name his daughter gave him suggests; but it is in no way abnormal. The discontinuities he perceived in himself are present in everyone. We are all bundles of sensations. The unified, continuous self that we encounter in everyday experience belongs in *maya*. We are programmed to perceive identity in ourselves, when in truth there is only change. We are hardwired for the illusion of self.

We cannot look steadily at the momentary world, for if we did we could not act. Nor can we observe the changes that are taking place incessantly in ourselves, for the self that witnesses them comes and goes in the blink of an eye. Selfhood is a side effect of the coarseness of consciousness; the inner life is too subtle and transient to be known to itself. But the sense of self has another source. Language begins in the play of animals and birds. So does the illusion of selfhood.

On watching two monkeys playing, Gregory Bateson wrote thus:

> ... this phenomenon, play, could only occur if the participant organisms were capable of some degree of meta-communication, i.e. of exchanging signals which would carry the message 'this is play'. ... Expanded, the statement 'This is play' looks something like this: 'These actions in which we now engage do not denote what those actions *for which they stand* would denote.'

Bateson concluded:

> Not only does the playful nip not denote what would be
> denoted by the bite for which it stands, but in addition,
> the bite itself is fictional. Not only do the playing animals
> not quite mean what they are saying, but they are usually
> communicating about something which does not exist.

Ravens have been recorded swooping over bands of gorillas, teasingly playing at attacking them. Again, they have
been observed pretending to make a cache in which to hide
food and then – when they believe they are unobserved –
secreting it elsewhere. These birds show the ability to deceive
that comes with the power of language. In this they are no
different from humans. Where humans differ from ravens is
that they use language to look back on their lives and call up
a virtual self.

The illusion of enduring selfhood arises with speech. We
acquire a sense of ourselves by our parents speaking to us in
infancy; our memories are strung together by many bodily
continuities, but also by our names; we contrive shifting his-
tories of ourselves in a fitful interior monologue; we form a
conception of having a lifetime ahead of us by using language to construct a variety of possible futures. By using
language we have invented a fictive self, which we project
into the past and the future – and even beyond the grave. The
self we imagine surviving death is a phantom even in life.

Our fictive selves are frail constructions. The sense of *I* is
dissolved or transformed in trance and dreams, weakened or

destroyed in fever and madness. It is in abeyance when we are absorbed in action. We may forget it in ecstasy or contemplation. But it always returns. The dissolution of self that mystics seek comes only with death.

The *I* is a thing of the moment, and yet our lives are ruled by it. We cannot rid ourselves of this inexistent thing. In our normal awareness of the present moment the sensation of selfhood is unshakeable. This is the primordial human error, in virtue of which we pass our lives as in a dream.

14

THE ULTIMATE DREAM

In Buddhist meditation, the adept peels away the veils of habit that shroud our senses by a practice of bare attention. Buddhists believe that by the refinement of attention we can attain insight into reality – the momentary, vanishing world that ordinary attention simplifies and makes palatable to us. In order to help us live, the mind censors the senses; but as a result we inhabit a world of shadows. As the contemporary Buddhist meditation teacher Gunaratana has put it: 'Our human perceptual habits are remarkably stupid. . . . We tune out 99 percent of the sensory stimuli we actually receive, and we solidify the remainder into discrete mental objects. Then we react to those mental objects in programmed habitual ways.'

The Buddhist ideal of awakening implies that we can sever our links with our evolutionary past. We can raise ourselves from the sleep in which other animals pass their lives. Our illusions dissolved, we need no longer suffer. This is only another doctrine of salvation, subtler than that of the Christians, but no different from Christianity in its goal of leaving our animal inheritance behind.

But the idea that we can rid ourselves of animal illusion is the greatest illusion of all. Meditation may give us a fresher view of things, but it cannot uncover them as they are in themselves. The lesson of evolutionary psychology and cognitive science is that we are descendants of a long lineage, only a fraction of which is human. We are far more than the traces that other humans have left in us. Our brains and spinal cords are encrypted with traces of far older worlds.

Even the deepest contemplation only recalls us to our unreality. Seeing that the self we take ourselves to be is illusory does not mean seeing through it to something else. It is more like surrendering to a dream. To see our selves as figments is to awake, not to reality, but to a lucid dream, a false awakening that has no end.

That we cannot awaken from our dream is recognised in Taoism. This indigenous Chinese folk religion encompasses many traditions: a popular cult of magic and ritual and meditative and sexual practices used by yogis and alchemists in the pursuit of longevity or immortality. The best-known Taoist text, the *Lao Tzu*, has been read in Western countries as a manual for mystics and anarchists. In fact it is more of an anthology, a hybrid collection of cryptic verses in which the barriers between logic and poetry melt away and an amoral manual emerges of statecraft and personal survival in troubled times. The other great Taoist collection, the *Chuang-Tzu*, parts of which may actually derive from a philosopher-poet who lived in China in the fourth century B.C., comes closer to being a mystical text. But the mystical vision it expresses is quite different from any found in Western countries, or in India.

Chuang-Tzu is as much a sceptic as a mystic. The sharp dichotomy between appearance and reality that is central in Buddhism is absent, and so is the attempt to transcend the illusions of everyday existence. Chuang-Tzu sees human life as a dream, but he does not seek to awaken from it. In a famous passage he writes of dreaming he was a butterfly, and not knowing on awakening whether he is a human being who has dreamt of being a butterfly, or a butterfly dreaming he is a human being:

> Once upon a time, I, Chuang-Tzu, dreamt I was a butterfly, flitting around and enjoying myself. I had no idea I was Chuang-Tzu. Then suddenly I woke up and was Chuang-Tzu again. But I could not tell, had I been Chuang-Tzu dreaming I was a butterfly, or a butterfly dreaming I was Chuang-Tzu? However, there must be some sort of difference between Chuang-Tzu and a butterfly! We call this the transformation of things.

Unlike the Buddha, A. C. Graham explains, Chuang-Tzu did not seek to awaken from the dream. He dreamt of dreaming more lucidly: 'Buddhists awaken out of dreaming; Chuang-Tzu wakes up *to* dreaming.' Awakening to the truth that life is a dream need not mean turning away from it. It may mean embracing it:

> If 'Life is a dream' implies that no achievement is lasting, it also implies that life can be charged with the wonder of dreams, that we drift spontaneously through events that follow a logic different from that of everyday intelligence, that fears and regrets are as unreal as hopes and desires.

Chuang-Tzu admits no idea of salvation. There is no self and no awakening from the dream of self:

> When we dream we do not know we are dreaming, and in the middle of a dream we interpret a dream within it; not until we wake do we know that we were dreaming. Only at the ultimate awakening shall we know that this is the ultimate dream.

We cannot be rid of illusions. Illusion is our natural condition. Why not accept it?

15

THE EXPERIMENT

Contemporary philosophers are not so bold as to claim that philosophy teaches us how to live, but they are hard put to say what it does teach. When pressed they may venture the opinion that it instils clarity of thinking. A worthy object, to be sure. But clear thought can be inculcated by the study of history, geography or physics. Rigour of mind should not need a university department of its own.

In the Middle Ages, philosophy gave an intellectual scaffolding to the Church; in the nineteenth and twentieth centuries it served a myth of progress. Today, serving neither religion nor a political faith, philosophy is a subject without a subject matter, scholasticism without the charm of dogma.

The ancient Greek philosophers had a practical aim — peace of mind. As it was practised by Socrates, 'philosophy' was not the mere pursuit of knowledge. It was a way of life, a culture of dialectical debate and an armoury of spiritual exercises, whose goal was not truth but tranquillity. Pyrrho — the founder of Greek Scepticism — did not need to go with Alexander to India to discover philosophies whose goal was inner peace. The ancient Greeks were at one with their contemporaries in India. For Sankara and Nagarjuna, as for Socrates and Plato, the goal of philosophy was the serenity that comes with freedom from the world. In China, the same was true of Yang Chu and Chuang-Tzu.

If philosophers have rarely considered the possibility that truth might not bring happiness, the reason is that truth has rarely been of the first importance to them. In that case, we are entitled to ask whether philosophy merits the authority it claims for itself, and how far it is qualified to sit in judgement over other ways of thinking. If happiness is what we are seeking, is it to be found in mere tranquillity? The Russian writer

Leo Shestov contrasted Spinoza's quest for peace of mind with Pascal's struggle for salvation:

> Philosophy sees the supreme good in a sleep which nothing can trouble. . . . That is why it is so careful to get rid of the incomprehensible, the enigmatic, and the mysterious; and avoids anxiously those questions to which it has already made answer. Pascal, on the other hand, sees in the inexplicable and incomprehensible nature of our surroundings the promise of a better existence, and every effort to simplify or to reduce the unknown to the known seems to him blasphemy.

Like the ancient Stoics before him, Spinoza sought relief from inner unrest; but what is so admirable in being ruled by a need for peace of mind? We need not share Pascal's fears or hopes to grasp the force of Shestov's question. If what is at issue is not truth but happiness and freedom, why must philosophy have the last word? Why should not faith and myth have equal rights?

Formerly philosophers sought peace of mind while pretending to seek the truth. Perhaps we should set ourselves a different aim: to discover which illusions we can give up, and which we will never shake off. We will still be seekers after truth, more so than in the past; but we will renounce the hope of a life without illusion. Henceforth our aim will be to identify our invincible illusions. Which untruths might we be rid of, and which can we not do without? – that is the question, that is the experiment.

3
THE VICES OF MORALITY

That man is the noblest creature may be inferred from the fact that no other creature has contested this claim.

G. C. LICHTENBERG

1

PORCELAIN AND THE PRICE OF LIFE

Utz lived indifferently through the worst years of his country's history. For him, the Nazi occupation of Czechoslovakia and the communist takeover that soon followed were opportunities to add to his collection of porcelain. All his human contacts served this passion. He was ready to collaborate with any regime so long as it helped him amass the beautiful objects he craved.

Utz's life seems strange to most of us, but what exactly is wrong with it? It is true that in many ways it is a poor one. It lacks deep friendship, abiding love or any commitment to a cause. But in these respects, how is it different from most people's lives? It is tempting to say that what marks Utz out from the common run of mankind is his amorality. He will do almost anything to get his hands on fine china – including coming to terms with the worst kinds of tyranny. But – once again – how does Utz differ from the majority of his fellow citizens? During the Nazi and communist periods they did what most people always do – they made their murky accommodations with power.

If you are like most people, you think of 'morality' as something special, a set of values that outweighs all others. No doubt fine china is worth a lot, but it counts for nothing when it comes into conflict with morality . . . Beauty is a wonderful thing, but not if it is purchased at the price of acting immorally . . . Morality, in other words, is extremely important . . . And yet, if you are like most other people but – unlike most people – you are honest with yourself, you will find that morality plays a far smaller part in your life than you have been taught that it should.

We inherit our belief – or pretence – that moral values take precedence over all other valuable things from a variety of sources, but chiefly from Christianity. In the Bible, morality is something that comes from beyond the world: right is what God commands, wrong what God forbids. And morality is more important than anything else – fine china, say, or good looks – because it is backed up by God's will. If you do wrong – that is, if you disobey God – you will be punished. Moral principles are not just rules of thumb for living well. They are imperatives which you must obey.

It may seem that this is a rather primitive view – one that has long been superseded. It is certainly primitive, but it is still very widely believed. Enlightenment humanists are as emphatic as old-time Christians that morality is supremely important. Philosophers are inordinately fond of asking why anyone should be moral, but somehow they never doubt that being moral is better than being anything else.

If Bruce Chatwin's novel *Utz* teaches any lesson, it is that the importance of morality in our lives is a fiction. We use it in the stories we tell ourselves and others about our lives to give them a sense they might otherwise lack. But in so doing we obscure the truth of how we live.

Moral philosophy has always been an exercise in make-believe, less realistic in its picture of human life than the average bourgeois novel. We must look elsewhere if we want anything that approaches the truth.

Here is a true story. A sixteen-year-old prisoner in a Nazi concentration camp was raped by a guard. Knowing that any prisoner who appeared without a cap on morning parade was immediately shot, the guard stole his victim's cap. The victim once shot, the rape could not be uncovered. The prisoner knew that his only chance of life was to find a cap. So he stole the cap of another camp inmate, asleep in bed, and lived to tell the tale. The other prisoner was shot.

Roman Frister, the prisoner who stole the cap, describes the death of his fellow inmate as follows:

> The officer and the kapo walked down the lines. . . . I counted the seconds as they counted the prisoners. I wanted it to be over. They were up to row four. The capless man didn't beg for his life. We all knew the rules of the game, the killers and the killed alike. There was no need for words. The shot rang out without warning. There was a short, dry, echoless thud. One bullet to the brain. They always shot you in the back of the skull. There was a war on. Ammunition had to be used sparingly. I didn't want to know who the man was. I was delighted to be alive.

What does morality say the young prisoner ought to have done? It says that human life has no price. Very well. Should he therefore have consented to lose his life? Or does the pricelessness of life mean that he was justified in doing anything to save his own? Morality is supposed to be universal and categorical. But the lesson of Roman Frister's story is that it is a convenience, to be relied upon only in normal times.

2

MORALITY AS SUPERSTITION

The idea of 'morality' as a set of laws has a biblical root. In the Old Testament, the good life means living according to God's will. But there is nothing that says that the laws given to the Jews apply universally. The idea that God's laws apply equally to everyone is a Christian invention.

The universal reach of Christianity is commonly seen as an advance on Judaism. In fact it was a step backwards. If there is one law binding on everyone, every way of life but one must be sinful.

It makes sense to think of ethics in terms of laws if – as in the Old Testament – it is a particular way of life that is being codified. But what sense is there in the idea of laws that apply to everyone? Isn't this idea of morality just an ugly superstition?

3

THE UNSANCTITY OF HUMAN LIFE

Having lost the skills of sewing, fishing and making fire, the indigenous people of Tasmania lived more simply than even Aboriginals on the Australian mainland from whom they had been isolated by rising sea levels around ten thousand years ago. When the ships bearing European settlers arrived in Tasmania in 1772, the indigenous people seem not to have noticed them. Unable to process a sight for which nothing had prepared them, they returned to their ways.

They had no defences against the settlers. By 1830 their numbers had been reduced from around five thousand to seventy-two. In the intervening years they had been used for slave labour and sexual pleasure, tortured and mutilated. They had been hunted like vermin and their skins had been sold for a government bounty. When the males were killed, female survivors were turned loose with the heads of their husbands tied around their necks. Males who were not killed were usually castrated. Children were clubbed to death. When the last indigenous Tasmanian male, William Lanner, died in 1869, his grave was opened by a member of the Royal Society of Tasmania, Dr George Stokell, who made a tobacco pouch from his skin. When the last 'fullblood' indigenous woman died a few years later, the genocide was complete.

Genocide is as human as art or prayer. This is not because humans are a uniquely aggressive species. The rate of violent death among some monkeys exceeds that among humans – if wars are excluded from the calculation; but as E. O. Wilson observes, 'if hamdryas baboons had nuclear weapons, they would destroy the world in a week'. Mass murder is a side effect of progress in technology. From the stone axe onwards, humans have used their tools to slaughter one another. Humans are weapon-making animals with an unquenchable fondness for killing.

Ancient history is testimony to the human taste for genocide. Jared Diamond writes:

> The wars of the Greeks and Trojans, of Rome and Carthage, and of the Assyrians and Babylonians and Persians proceeded to a common end: the slaughter of the defeated irrespective of sex, or else the killing of the men and the enslavement of the women.

In more modern times genocide is no less frequent. Between 1492 and 1990 there were at least thirty-six genocides claiming between tens of thousands and tens of millions of lives. Since 1950 there have been nearly twenty genocides; at least three of them had over a million victims (in Bangladesh, Cambodia and Rwanda).

The good Christian men and women who colonised Tasmania did not let their deep belief in the sanctity of human life stand in the way of their drive for *Lebensraum*. A century later, the strength of Christianity in Europe did not prevent it being the site for the most far-reaching genocide ever attempted. It is not the numbers killed in the Holocaust

that make it a crime without parallel. It was its goal of erad-
icating an entire culture. Hitler planned a Museum of Jewish
Culture, to be sited in Prague – a Museum of an Extinct
People.

This Nazi project was dealt with by Arthur Koestler in his
wartime novel *Arrival and Departure*. Koestler gives one of its
characters, a philosophising Nazi of a kind that really existed
in many parts of Europe at that time, a speech giving full vent
to Nazi aims:

> We have embarked on something – something gran-
> diose and gigantic beyond imagination. There are no
> more impossibilities for man now. For the first time we
> are attacking the biological structure of the race. We
> have started to breed a new species of *homo sapiens*.
> We have practically finished the task of exterminating
> or sterilising the gipsies in Europe; the liquidation of
> the Jews will be completed in a year or two. Personally
> I am fond of gipsy music and a clever Jew amuses me in
> a way; but we had to get rid of the nomadic gene, with
> its asocial and anarchic components, in the human
> chromosome. . . . We are the first to make use of the
> hypodermic syringe, the lancet and the sterilizing appa-
> ratus in our revolution.

This murderous vision was not confined to Nazis. In less vir-
ulent forms, the same view of human possibilities was held in
the thirties by much of the progressive intelligentsia. There
were some who found positive features even in national

socialism. For George Bernard Shaw, Nazi Germany was not a reactionary dictatorship but a legitimate heir to the European Enlightenment.

Nazism was a rag-bag of ideas, including occultist philosophies that rejected modern science. But it is mistaken to view it as unambiguously hostile to the Enlightenment. Inasmuch as it was a movement dedicated to toleration and personal freedom, Hitler loathed the Enlightenment. At the same time, like Nietzsche he shared the Enlightenment's vast hopes for humanity. Through positive and negative eugenics – breeding high-quality people and eliminating those judged inferior – humanity would become capable of the enormous tasks ahead of it. Shaking off the moral traditions of the past and purified by science, humankind would be master of the Earth. Shaw's view of Nazism was not so far-fetched. It chimed with Hitler's self-image as a fearless progressive and modernist.

Shaw viewed both the Soviet Union and Nazi Germany as progressive regimes. As such, he held, they were entitled to kill off obstructive or superfluous people. Throughout his life, the great playwright argued in favour of mass extermination as an alternative to imprisonment. It was better to kill the socially useless, he urged, than to waste public money locking them up.

This was not just a Shavian jest. At a party in honour of his seventy-fifth birthday held in Moscow during his visit to the USSR in August 1930, Shaw told his half-famished audience that when they learnt he was going to Russia his friends had loaded him up with tinned food; but – he joked – he threw it all out of the window in Poland before he reached the Soviet frontier. Shaw taunted his audience in full knowledge of their circumstances. He knew the Soviet famines were artificial. But he turned a jovial eye on their victims from the considered conviction that mass extermination was justified if it advanced the cause of progress.

Most Western observers lacked Shaw's clear-sightedness. They could not admit that the largest mass murder in modern times – perhaps in all of human history – was occurring in a progressive regime. Between 1917 and 1959 over 60 million people were killed in the Soviet Union. These mass murders were not concealed: they were public policy. Heller and Nekrich write:

> There is no question that the Soviet people knew about the massacres in the countryside. In fact, no one tried to conceal it. Stalin spoke openly about the 'liquidation of the kulaks as a class', and all his lieutenants echoed him. At the railroad stations, city dwellers could see the thousands of women and children who had fled from the villages and were dying from hunger.

It is sometimes asked why Western observers were so slow in recognising the truth about the Soviet Union. The reason is not that it was hard to come by. It was clear from hundreds of books by émigré survivors – and from statements by the Soviets themselves. But the facts were too uncomfortable for Western observers to admit. For the sake of their peace of mind they had to deny what they knew or suspected to be true. Like the Tasmanian Aboriginals who could not see the tall ships that brought their end, these *bien-pensants* could not bring themselves to see that the pursuit of progress had ended in mass murder.

'The scale of man-made death is the central moral and material fact of our time,' writes Gil Elliot. What makes the twentieth century special is not the fact that it is littered with massacres. It is the scale of its killings and the fact that they were premeditated for the sake of vast projects of world improvement.

Progress and mass murder run in tandem. As the numbers killed by famine and plague have waned, so death by violence has increased. As science and technology have advanced, so has proficiency in killing. As the hope for a better world has grown, so has mass murder.

4

CONSCIENCE

On Sunday afternoon, 23 April 1899, more than two thousand white Georgians, some of then arriving on a special excursion train, assembled near the town of Newman to witness the execution of Sam Hose, a black Georgian. Whole families turned up to watch. Parents sent notes to school asking teachers to excuse their children. Postcards were sent to those who could not attend the spectacle, and photographs were taken to preserve it in memory.

After learning of the death of her husband at one such occasion, Mary Turner – a black woman in her eighth month of pregnancy – swore to find those responsible and have them punished. A mob assembled and determined to teach her a lesson. After tying her ankles together they hung her from a tree upside down. While she was still alive her abdomen was cut open with a knife. The infant fell from her womb and its head was crushed by a member of the crowd. Then, as hundreds of bullets were fired into her body, Mary Turner was killed.

Were the smiling children who were photographed watching such events gnawed by remorse for the rest of their days? Or did they recall them with nostalgia and quiet satisfaction?

It has long been known that those who perform great acts of kindness are rarely forgiven. The same is true of those who suffer irreparable wrongs. When will Jews be forgiven the Holocaust?

Morality tells us that conscience may not be heard – but that it speaks always against cruelty and injustice. In fact conscience blesses cruelty and injustice – so long as their victims can be quietly buried.

5

THE DEATH OF TRAGEDY

Hegel wrote that tragedy is the collision of right with right. It is true that there is tragedy when weighty obligations are irreconcilably at odds, for then whatever we do contains wrong. Even so, tragedy has nothing to do with morality.

As a recognisable genre, tragedy begins with Homer, but tragedy was not born in the songs we read today in the *Iliad*. It came into the world with the masked figures, hybrids of animals and gods, who celebrated the cycle of nature in archaic festivals. Tragedy was born in the chorus that sang the mythic life and death of Dionysus. According to Gimbutas, 'A liturgical use of masked participants, the *thiasotes* or *tragoi*, led ultimately to their appearance on the stage and to the birth of tragedy.'

Tragedy is born of myth, not morality. Prometheus and Icarus are tragic heroes. Yet none of the myths in which they appear has anything to do with moral dilemmas. Nor have the greatest Greek tragedies.

If Euripides is the most tragic of the Greek playwrights, it is not because he deals with moral conflicts but because he understood that reason cannot be the guide of life. Euripides rejected the belief that Socrates made the basis of philosophy: that, as Dodds puts it, 'moral, like intellectual error, can arise only from a failure to use the reason we possess; and that when it does arise it must, like intellectual error, be curable by intellectual process'.

Like Homer, Euripides was a stranger to the faith that knowledge, goodness and happiness are one and the same. For both, tragedy came from the encounter of human will with fate. Socrates destroyed that archaic view of things. Reason enabled us to avoid disaster, or else it showed that disaster does not matter. This is what Nietzsche meant when he wrote that Socrates caused 'the death of tragedy'.

The pith of tragedy is not the collision of right with right. There is tragedy when humans refuse to submit to circumstances that neither courage nor intelligence can remedy. Tragedy befalls those who have wagered against the odds. The worth of their goals is irrelevant. The life of a petty criminal can be tragic, while that of a world statesman may be petty.

In our time, Christians and humanists have come together to make tragedy impossible. For Christians, tragedies are only blessings in disguise: the world – as Dante put it – is a divine comedy; there is an afterlife in which all tears will be wiped away. For humanists, we can look forward to a time when all people have the chance of a happy life; in the meantime, tragedy is an edifying reminder of how we can thrive in misfortune. But it is only in sermons or on the stage that human beings are ennobled by extremes of suffering.

Varlam Shalamov, according to the gulag survivor Gustaw Herling 'a writer before whom all the gulag literati, Solzhenitsyn included, must bow their heads', was first arrested in 1929 when he was only twenty-two and still a law student at Moscow University. He was sentenced to three years' hard labour in Solovki, an island that had been converted from an Orthodox monastery into a Soviet concentration camp. In 1937 he was again arrested and sentenced to five years in Kolyma, in northeastern Siberia. At a conservative estimate, around 3 million people perished in these Arctic camps and one third or more of the prisoners died each year.

Shalamov spent seventeen years in Kolyma. His book *Kolyma Tales* is written in a spare, Chekhovian style, with none of the didactic tones of Solzhenitsyn's works. Yet in occasional terse asides, and between the lines, there is a message: 'whoever thinks that he can behave differently has never touched the true bottom of life; he has never had to breathe his last in "a world without heroes"'.

Kolyma was a place in which morality had ceased to exist. In what Shalamov drily called 'literary fairy tales', deep human bonds are forged under the pressure of tragedy and need; but in fact no tie of friendship or sympathy was strong enough to survive life in Kolyma: 'If tragedy and need brought people together and gave birth to their friendship, then the need was not extreme and the tragedy not great,' Shalamov wrote. With all meaning drained from their lives, it might seem that the prisoners had no reason to go on; but most were too weak to seize the chances that came from time to time to end their lives in a way they had chosen: 'There are times when a man has to hurry so as not to lose his will to die.' Broken by hunger and cold, they moved insensibly to a senseless death.

Shalamov wrote: 'There is much there that a man should not know, should not see, and if he does see it, it is better for him to die.' After his return from the camps, he spent the remainder of his life refusing to forget what he had seen. Describing his journey back to Moscow, he wrote:

It was as if I had just awakened from a dream that had lasted for years. And suddenly I was afraid and felt a cold sweat from on my body. I was frightened by the terrible strength of man, his desire and ability to forget.

I realised I was ready to forget everything, to cross out twenty years of my life. And when I understood this, I conquered myself, I knew I would not permit my memory to forget everything that I had seen. And I regained my calm and fell asleep.

At its worst human life is not tragic but unmeaning. The soul is broken, but life lingers on. As the will fails, the mask of tragedy falls aside. What remains is only suffering. The last sorrow cannot be told. If the dead could speak we would not understand them. We are wise to hold to the semblance of tragedy; the truth unveiled would only blind us. As Czeslaw Milosz wrote:

> No-one with
> Impunity gives himself the eyes of a god.

Shalamov was released from Kolyma in 1951, but forbidden to leave the area. In 1953 he was allowed to leave Siberia but forbidden to live in a large city. He returned to Moscow in 1956 to find that his wife had left him and his daughter had rejected him. On his seventy-fifth birthday, living alone in an old people's home, blind and nearly deaf and speaking with great difficulty, he dictated several short poems to his one friend who occasionally visited him, which were published abroad. As a result, he was taken from the old people's home and, resisting all the while – perhaps believing he was being sent back to Kolyma – he was placed in a psychiatric hospital. Three days later, on 17 January 1982, he died in 'a small room with bars on the windows, facing a padded door with a round spy-hole'.

6

JUSTICE AND FASHION

Socratic philosophy and Christian religion encourage the belief that justice is timeless. In fact few ideas are more ephemeral.

John Rawls's theory of justice has dominated Anglo-American philosophy for a generation. It seeks to develop an account of justice that works only with widely accepted moral intuitions of fairness and relies at no point on controversial positions in ethics. The fruit of this modesty is a pious commentary on conventional moral beliefs.

Followers of Rawls avoid inspecting their moral intuitions too closely. Perhaps this is just as well. If they scrutinised them, they would find they had a history – often a rather short history. Today everyone knows that inequality is wrong. A century ago everyone knew that gay sex was wrong. The intuitions people have on moral questions are intensely felt. They are also shallow and transient to the last degree.

The egalitarian beliefs on which Rawls's theory is founded are like the sexual mores that were once believed to be the core of morality. The most local and changeable of things, they are revered as the very essence of morality.

As conventional opinion moves on, the current egalitarian consensus will be followed by a new orthodoxy, equally certain that it embodies unchanging moral truth.

Justice is an artefact of custom. Where customs are unsettled its dictates soon become dated. Ideas of justice are as timeless as fashions in hats.

7

WHAT EVERY WELL-BRED ENGLISHMAN KNOWS

George Bernard Shaw wrote somewhere that a well-bred Englishman knows nothing of the world – except the difference between right and wrong. The same could be said of pretty well all moral philosophers. Like the well-bred Englishmen of whom Shaw wrote, they think their ignorance is a virtue.

8

PSYCHOANALYSIS AND MORAL LUCK

We inherit from the thinkers of the Enlightenment the faith that anyone can be good. Yet this is not a conclusion that could be drawn from the work of the twentieth century's greatest Enlightenment thinker. The upshot of Freud's work is that being a good person is a matter of chance.

Freud taught that for any human being kindness or cruelty, having a sense of justice or lacking it, depend on the accidents of childhood. We all know this to be true, but it goes against much of what we say we believe. We cannot give up the pretence that being good is something anyone can achieve. If we did, we would have to admit that, like beauty and intelligence, goodness is a gift of fortune. We would have to accept that, in the parts of our lives where we are most attached to it, freedom of the will is an illusion. We would have to own up to what we all deny – that being good is good luck. By making us face this awkward truth, Freud wounded the concept of 'morality' more deeply than did Nietzsche.

9

MORALITY AS AN APHRODISIAC

A sense of guilt may add spice to otherwise unremarkable vices. There are undoubtedly those who have converted to Christianity because they seek an excitement that mere pleasure can no longer supply. Think of Graham Greene, who used the sense of sin he acquired through converting to Catholicism as an aphrodisiac. Morality has hardly made us better people; but it has certainly enriched our vices.

Post-Christians deny themselves the pleasures of guilt. They blush at using a queasy conscience to flavour their stale pleasures. As a result, they are notably lacking in *joie de vivre*. Among those who have once been Christians, pleasure can be intense only if it is mixed with the sensation of acting immorally.

10

A WEAKNESS FOR PRUDENCE

Philosophers from Socrates onwards have never tired of asking why anyone should be moral. A more interesting question is why anyone should be prudent. Why should I care what becomes of me in future?

Philosophers have always had a weakness for prudence. From Socrates onwards they have laboured to show that the truly prudent person will always act morally. They would have been better employed questioning self-interest.

Why should my future goals matter more than those I have now? It is not just that they are remote – even hypothetical. They may be less worth striving for: 'Why should a youth suppress his budding passions in favour of the sordid interests of his own withered old age? Why is that problematical old man who may bear his name fifty years hence nearer to him now than any other imaginary creature?'

We need not share George Santayana's view of old age to see that his question is unanswerable. Caring about your self as it will be in the future is no more reasonable than caring about the self you are now. Less so, if your future self is less worth caring about.

11

SOCRATES, INVENTOR OF MORALITY

It may be that Socrates was not the questioning rationalist Plato made him out to be. He may have been a playful sophist who looked on philosophy as sport, a game no one took seriously – least of all himself. Yet under Socrates's influence ethics ceased to be the art of living well in a dangerous world – as it had been for Homer. It became the search for a super-good that nothing can destroy, a uniquely potent value that defeats all others and insures those who live by it against tragedy.

In the Greek world in which Homer's songs were sung, it was taken for granted that everyone's life is ruled by fate and chance. For Homer, human life is a succession of contingencies: all good things are vulnerable to fortune. Socrates could not accept this archaic tragic vision. He believed that virtue and happiness were one and the same: nothing can harm a truly good man. So he re-envisioned the good to make it indestructible. Beyond the goods of human life – health, beauty, pleasure, friendship, life itself – there was a Good that surpassed them all. In Plato, this became the idea of the Form of the Good, the mystical fusion of all values into a harmonious spiritual whole – an idea later absorbed into the Christian conception of God. But the idea that ethics is concerned with a kind of value that is beyond contingency, that can somehow prevail over any kind of loss or misfortune, came from Socrates. It was he who invented 'morality'.

We think of morality as a set of laws or rules that everyone must obey, and as a special sort of value, which takes precedence over every other. Morality consists of these prejudices, which we inherit partly from Christianity and partly from classical Greek philosophy.

In the world of Homer, there was no morality. There were surely ideas of right and wrong. But there was no idea of a set of rules that everyone must follow, or of a special, superpotent kind of value that defeats all others. Ethics was about virtues such as courage and wisdom; but even the bravest and wisest of men go down to defeat and ruin.

We prefer to found our lives – in public, at least – on the pretence that 'morality' wins out in the end. Yet we do not really believe it. At bottom, we know that nothing can make us proof against fate and chance. In this, we are closer to the archaic, pre-Socratic Greeks than we are to classical Greek philosophy.

12

IMMORAL MORALITY

Humans thrive in conditions that morality condemns. The peace and prosperity of one generation stand on the injustices of earlier generations; the delicate sensibilities of liberal societies are fruits of war and empire. The same is true of individuals. Gentleness flourishes in sheltered lives; an instinctive trust in others is rarely strong in people who have struggled against the odds. The qualities we say we value above all others cannot withstand ordinary life. Happily, we do not value them as much as we say we do. Much that we admire comes from things we judge to be evil or wrong. This is true of morality itself.

Machiavelli's *The Prince* has long been condemned for preaching immorality. It teaches that anyone who tries to be honourable in the struggle for power will surely come to grief: winning and keeping power requires *virtu*, boldness and a talent for dissimulation. (Machiavelli's teaching is scandalous even today, when everyone wants to be a prince.) Hobbes's *Leviathan* was attacked for observing that, in war, force and fraud are virtues. The lesson of Bernard de Mandeville's *The Fable of the Bees* is that prosperity is driven by vice – by greed, vanity and envy. If Nietzsche still has the power to shock, it is because he showed that some of the virtues we most admire are sublimations of motives – such as cruelty and resentment – we most strongly condemn.

In these writers a forbidden truth is made plain. It is not only that the good life has very little to do with 'morality'. It flourishes only because of 'immorality'.

Moral philosophers have always evaded this truth. Aristotle began the evasion when he presented his doctrine of the Mean, which says that the virtues wax and wane together. Courage and prudence, justice and sympathy – all are highly developed in the best man. (Let us not forget that Aristotle speaks only of males.) But, as even Aristotle must have noticed, virtues can be rivals: a rigorous sense of justice can drive out sympathy. Worse, 'virtue' may depend on 'vice';

courage often goes with a certain recklessness. Where vice and virtue are concerned, human beings are not all of one piece.

Moral philosophy is very largely a branch of fiction. Despite this, a philosopher has yet to write a great novel. The fact should not be surprising. In philosophy the truth about human life is of no interest.

13

THE FETISH OF CHOICE

For us, nothing is more important than to live as we choose. This is not because we value freedom more than people did in earlier times. It is because we have identified the good life with the chosen life.

For the pre-Socratic Greeks, the fact that our lives are framed by limits was what makes us human. Being born a mortal, in a given place and time, strong or weak, swift or slow, brave or cowardly, beautiful or ugly, suffering tragedy or being spared it – these features of our lives are given to us, they cannot be chosen. If the Greeks could have imagined a life without them, they could not have recognised it as that of a human being.

The ancient Greeks were right. The ideal of the chosen life does not square with how we live. We are not authors of our lives; we are not even part-authors of the events that mark us most deeply. Nearly everything that is most important in our lives is unchosen. The time and place we are born, our parents, the first language we speak – these are chance, not choice. It is the casual drift of things that shapes our most fateful relationships. The life of each of us is a chapter of accidents.

Personal autonomy is the work of our imagination, not the way we live. Yet we have been thrown into a time in which everything is provisional. New technologies alter our lives daily. The traditions of the past cannot be retrieved. At the same time we have little idea of what the future will bring. We are forced to live as if we were free.

The cult of choice reflects the fact that we must improvise our lives. That we cannot do otherwise is a mark of our unfreedom. Choice has become a fetish; but the mark of a fetish is that it is unchosen.

14

ANIMAL VIRTUES

If you seek the origins of ethics, look to the lives of other animals. The roots of ethics are in the animal virtues. Humans cannot live well without virtues they share with their animal kin.

This is not a new idea. Two and a half thousand years ago, Aristotle observed the similarities between humans and dolphins. Like humans, dolphins act purposefully to achieve the goods things of life, they take pleasure in exercising their powers and skills, and they display qualities such as curiosity and bravery. Humans are not alone in having an ethical life. In thinking this way, Aristotle was at one with Nietzsche, who wrote:

> The beginnings of justice, as of prudence, moderation, bravery – in short, of all that we designate as the *Socratic virtues* – are *animal*: a consequence of that drive which teaches us to seek food and elude enemies. Now if we consider that even the highest human being has only become more elevated and subtle in the nature of his food and in his conception of what is inimical to him, it is not improper to describe the entire phenomenon of morality as animal.

The dominant Western view is different. It teaches that humans are unlike other animals, which simply respond to the situations in which they find themselves. We can scrutinise our motives and impulses; we can know why we act as we do. By becoming ever more self-aware, we can approach a point at which our actions are the results of our choices. When we are fully conscious, everything we do will be done for reasons we can know. At that point, we will be authors of our lives.

This may seem fantastical, and so it is. Yet it is what we are taught by Socrates, Aristotle and Plato, Descartes, Spinoza and Marx. For all of them, consciousness is our very essence, and the good life means living as a fully conscious individual.

The fact that we are not autonomous subjects deals a death blow to morality – but it is the only possible ground of ethics. If we were not made up of fragments we could not practise self-deception or suffer from weakness of will. If choice ruled our lives we could never display spontaneous generosity. If our selves were as fixed as we imagine them to be, we could not cope with a world abounding in discontinuities. If we were truly monads, each locked up in himself, we could not have the fugitive empathy with other living things that is the ultimate source of ethics.

Western thought is fixated on the gap between what *is* and what *ought to be*. But in everyday life we do not scan our options beforehand, then enact the one that is best. We simply deal with whatever is at hand. We get up in the morning and put on our clothes without meaning to do so. We help a friend in just the same way. Different people follow different customs; but in acting without intention, we are not simply following habit. Intentionless acts occur in all sorts of situations, including those we have never come across before.

Outside the Western tradition, the Taoists of ancient China saw no gap between *is* and *ought*. Right action was whatever comes from a clear view of the situation. They did not follow moralists – in their day, Confucians – in wanting to fetter human beings with rules or principles. For Taoists, the good life is only the natural life lived skilfully. It has no particular purpose. It has nothing to do with the will, and it does not consist in trying to realise any ideal. Everything we do can be done more or less well; but if we act well it is not because we translate our intentions into deeds. It is because we deal skilfully with whatever needs to be done. The good life means living according to our natures and circumstances. There is nothing that says that it is bound to be the same for everybody, or that it must conform with 'morality'.

In Taoist thought, the good life comes spontaneously; but spontaneity is far from simply acting on the impulses that occur to us. In Western traditions such as Romanticism, spontaneity is linked with subjectivity. In Taoism it means acting dispassionately, on the basis of an objective view of the situation at hand. The common man cannot see things objectively, because his mind is clouded by anxiety about achieving his goals. Seeing clearly means not projecting our goals into the world; acting spontaneously means acting according to the needs of the situation. Western moralists will ask what is the purpose of such action, but for Taoists the good life has no purpose. It is like swimming in a whirlpool, responding to the currents as they come and go. 'I enter with the inflow, and emerge with the outflow, follow the Way of the water, and do not impose my selfishness upon it. This is how I stay afloat in it,' says the *Chuang-Tzu*.

In this view, ethics is simply a practical skill, like fishing or swimming. The core of ethics is not choice or conscious awareness, but the knack of knowing what to do. It is a skill that comes with practice and an empty mind. A. C. Graham explains:

The Taoist relaxes the body, calms the mind, loosens the grip of categories made habitual by naming, frees the current of thought for more fluid differentiations and assimilations, and instead of pondering choices lets his problems solve themselves as inclination spontaneously finds its own direction. . . . He does not have to make decisions based on standards of good and bad because, granted only that enlightenment is better than ignorance, it is self-evident that among spontaneous inclinations the one prevailing in greatest clarity of mind, other things being equal, will be best, the one in accord with the Way.

Few human beings have the knack of living well. Observing this, the Taoists looked to other animals as their guides to the good life. Animals in the wild know how to live; they do not need to think or choose. It is only when they are fettered by humans that they cease to live naturally.

As the *Chuang-Tzu* puts it, horses, when they live wild, eat grass and drink water; when they are content, they entwine their necks and rub each other. When angry, they turn their backs on each other and kick out. This is what horses know. But if harnessed together and lined up under constraints, they know how to look sideways and to arch their necks, to career around and try to spit out the bit and rid themselves of the reins.

For people in thrall to 'morality', the good life means perpetual striving. For Taoists it means living effortlessly, according to our natures. The freest human being is not one who acts on reasons he has chosen for himself, but one who never has to choose. Rather than agonising over alternatives, he responds effortlessly to situations as they arise. He lives not as he chooses but as he must. Such a human being has the perfect freedom of a wild animal – or a machine. As the *Lieh-Tzu* says: 'The highest man at rest is as though dead, in movement is like a machine. He knows neither why he is at rest nor why he is not, why he is in movement nor why he is not.'

The idea that freedom means becoming like a wild animal or machine is offensive to Western religious and humanist prejudices, but it is consistent with the most advanced scientific knowledge. A. C. Graham explains:

Taoism coincides with the scientific worldview at just those points where the latter most disturbs westerners rooted in the Christian tradition – the littleness of man in a vast universe; the inhuman Tao which all things follow, without purpose and indifferent to human needs; the transience of life, the impossibility of knowing what comes after death; unending change in which the possibility of progress is not even conceived; the relativity of values; a fatalism very close to determinism; even a suggestion that the human organism operates like a machine.

Autonomy means acting on reasons I have chosen; but the lesson of cognitive science is that there is no self to do the choosing. We are far more like machines and wild animals than we imagine. But we cannot attain the amoral selflessness of wild animals, or the choiceless automatism of machines. Perhaps we can learn to live more lightly, less burdened by morality. We cannot return to a purely spontaneous existence.

If humans differ from other animals, it is partly in the conflicts of their instincts. They crave security, but they are easily bored; they are peace-loving animals, but they have an itch for violence; they are drawn to thinking, but at the same time they hate and fear the unsettlement thinking brings. There is no way of life in which all these needs can be satisfied. Luckily, as the history of philosophy testifies, humans have a gift for self-deception, and thrive in ignorance of their natures.

Morality is a sickness peculiar to humans, the good life is a refinement of the virtues of animals. Arising from our animal natures, ethics needs no ground; but it runs aground in the conflicts of our needs.

4
THE UNSAVED

The certitude that there is no salvation is a form of salvation, in fact it *is* salvation. Starting from here, one might organise our own life as well as construct a philosophy of history: the insoluble as solution, as the only way out.

E. M. CIORAN

1

SAVIOURS

The Buddha promised release from something we all understand – suffering. By contrast, no one can say what was humankind's original sin, and no one understands how the suffering of Christ can redeem it.

Christianity began as a Jewish sect. For the early followers of Jesus, sin meant disobedience to God, and the punishment for sinful mankind was the end of the world. These mythic beliefs were linked with the figure of a messiah, a divine messenger who brought retribution to the world and redemption to the obedient few.

It was Saint Paul, not Jesus, who founded Christianity. Paul turned a Jewish messianic cult into a Greco-Roman mystery religion; but he could not free the faith he invented from Jesus's inheritance. It is not only that beliefs about sin and redemption were at the heart of Jesus's teaching. Without some such beliefs, the Christian promise of redemption has no meaning. If we are not sinners we do not need to be redeemed, and the promise of redemption cannot help us endure our sorrows. As Borges writes of Jesus:

> Night has fallen. He has died now.
> A fly crawls over the still flesh.
> Of what use is it to me that this man has suffered,
> If I am suffering now?

In D. H. Lawrence's story *The Escaped Cock*, Jesus comes back from the dead only to give up the idea of saving mankind. He views the world with wonder and asks himself: 'From what, and to what, could this infinite whirl be saved?'

Humans think they are free, conscious beings, when in truth they are deluded animals. At the same time they never cease trying to escape from what they imagine themselves to be. Their religions are attempts to be rid of a freedom they have never possessed. In the twentieth century, the utopias of Right and Left served the same function. Today, when politics is unconvincing even as entertainment, science has taken on the role of mankind's deliverer.

One may imagine an esoteric teaching that says there is nothing from which to seek deliverance, a teaching whose aim is to free humanity from the yoke of salvation. In *Report to Greco*, Nikos Kazantzakis has the Buddha telling his faithful disciple Ananda:

> Whoever says salvation exists is a slave, because he keeps weighing each of his words and deeds at every moment. 'Will I be saved or damned?' he tremblingly asks. . . .

Salvation means deliverance from all saviours . . . now you understand who is the perfect Saviour. . . . It is the Saviour who shall deliver mankind from salvation.

A pretty notion, but who needs it? Animals like any other, but more restless than most, humans find fulfilment, in Robinson Jeffers's words:

> in the
> Disastrous rhythm, the heavy and mobile masses,
>   the dance of the
> Dream-led masses down the dark mountain.

Average humanity takes its saviours too lightly to need saving from them. Its would-be deliverers need it more than it needs them. When it looks to its deliverers it is for distraction, not salvation.

2

THE GRAND INQUISITOR AND FLYING FISH

In his commentary on Dostoevsky's parable of the Grand Inquisitor, D. H. Lawrence confessed that he had once rejected the philosophy of the Grand Inquisitor as a 'cynical-satanical pose'. In Dostoevsky's parable, which appears as a 'poem' composed by Ivan Karamazov and told to his brother Aloysha in the novel *The Brothers Karamazov*, Jesus returns to the world during the time of the Spanish Inquisition. Though he comes 'softly, unobserved', it is not long before he is recognised by the people, and taken prisoner by the Grand Inquisitor. Shut up in the ancient palace of the Holy Inquisition, he is questioned, but refuses to answer.

The Grand Inquisitor tells Jesus that humanity is too weak to bear the gift of freedom. It does not seek freedom but bread – not the divine bread promised by Jesus, but ordinary earthly bread. People will worship whomever gives them bread, for they need their rulers to be gods. The Grand Inquisitor tells Jesus that his teaching has been amended to deal with humanity as it really is: 'We have corrected Thy work and have founded it on *miracle, mystery* and *authority*. And men rejoiced that they were again led like sheep, and that the terrible gift that brought them such suffering was, at last, lifted from their hearts.'

Lawrence tells us he once dismissed the Grand Inquisitor's assertion that humans cannot bear freedom as 'showing off in blasphemy'. On reflection, his judgement was different: the Grand Inquisitor's assertion contains 'the final and unanswerable criticism of Christ . . . it is a deadly, devastating summing-up, unanswerable because borne out by the long experience of humanity. It is reality versus illusion, and the illusion was Jesus's, while time itself retorts with the reality.' Lawrence explains his change of mind with a question: 'Is it true that mankind demands, and will always demand, miracle, mystery and authority?' He answers:

Surely it is true. Today, man gets his sense of the miraculous from science and machinery, radio, airplanes, vast ships, zeppelins, poison gas, artificial silk: these things nourish man's sense of the miraculous as magic did in the past. . . . Dostoevsky's diagnosis of human nature is simple and unanswerable. We have to submit, and agree that men are like that.

Lawrence was right. Today, for the mass of humanity, science and technology embody 'miracle, mystery and authority'. Science promises that the most ancient human fantasies will at last be realised. Sickness and ageing will be abolished; scarcity and poverty will be no more; the species will become immortal. Like Christianity in the past, the modern cult of science lives on the hope of miracles. But to think that science can transform the human lot is to believe in magic. Time retorts to the illusions of humanism with the reality: frail, deranged, undelivered humanity. Even as it enables poverty to be diminished and sickness to be alleviated, science will be used to refine tyranny and perfect the art of war.

The truth that Dostoevsky puts in the mouth of the Grand Inquisitor is that humankind has never sought freedom, and never will. The secular religions of modern times tell us that humans yearn to be free; and it is true that they find restraint of any kind irksome. Yet it is rare that individuals value their freedom more than the comfort that comes with servility, and rarer still for whole peoples to do so. As Joseph de Maistre commented on Rousseau's dictum that men are born free but are everywhere in chains: to think that, because a few people sometimes seek freedom, all human beings want it is like thinking that, because there are flying fish, it is in the nature of fish to fly.

No doubt there will be free societies in the future as there have been in the past. But they will be rare, and variations on anarchy and tyranny will be the norm. The needs that are met by tyrants are as real as those to which freedom answers; sometimes they are more urgent. Tyrants promise security – and release from the tedium of everyday existence. To be sure, this is only a confused fantasy. The drab truth of tyranny is a life spent in waiting. But the perennial romance of tyranny comes from its promising its subjects a life more interesting than any they can contrive for themselves. Whatever they become, tyrannies begin as festivals of the depressed. Dictators may come to power on the back of chaos, but their unspoken promise is that they will relieve the boredom of their subjects. On this, the Grand Inquisitor cannot be faulted.

The lie in the Grand Inquisitor's speech is his view of himself. He sees himself as the most tragic of men, cursed with a vision of truth denied to feeble humanity, and so burdened with the responsibility of caring for it. He is bound to save humanity from 'the great anxiety and terrible agony they endure at present in making a free decision for themselves. And all will be happy, all the millions of creatures except the hundred thousand who rule over them. For only we, we who guard the mystery, will be unhappy.' This is only Romantic conceit run wild. The Grand Inquisitor's vigil cannot bring salvation to humanity. It does not need it. It can only bring peace to the Grand Inquisitor himself.

In fact, of course, there are no Grand Inquisitors. The inquisitors on whom Dostoevsky's character was modelled were not saints who dedicated their lives to sparing humanity from being crushed by the truth. They were no different from the rest of mankind, perhaps even worse: crazed fanatics, revenge seekers or timorous careerists. Dostoevsky's lurid portrait is belied by the human reality. Inquisitors are made not from the saintly-satanic urge to spare mankind from truth, but from fear, resentment and the pleasure of bullying the weak.

Science can advance human knowledge, it cannot make humanity cherish truth. Like the Christians of former times, scientists are caught up in the web of power; they struggle for survival and success; their view of the world is a patchwork of conventional beliefs. Science cannot bring 'miracle, mystery and authority' to humankind, if only because – like those who served the Church in the past – its servants are all too human.

3

IN PRAISE OF POLYTHEISM

No polytheist ever imagined that all of humankind would come to live in the same way, for polytheists took for granted that humans would always worship different gods. Only with

Christianity did the belief take root that one way of life could be lived by everyone.

For polytheists, religion is a matter of practice, not belief; and there are many kinds of practice. For Christians, religion is a matter of true belief. If only one belief can be true, every way of life in which it is not accepted must be in error.

Polytheists may be jealous of their gods, but they are not missionaries. Without monotheism, humankind would surely still have been one of the most violent animals, but it would have been spared wars of religion. If the world had remained polytheist, it could not have produced communism or 'global democratic capitalism'.

It is pleasant to dream of a world without militant faiths, religious or political. Pleasant, but idle. Polytheism is too delicate a way of thinking for modern minds.

4

ATHEISM, THE LAST CONSEQUENCE OF CHRISTIANITY

Unbelief is a move in a game whose rules are set by believers. To deny the existence of God is to accept the categories of monotheism. As these categories fall into disuse, unbelief becomes uninteresting, and soon it is meaningless. Atheists say they want a secular world, but a world defined by the absence of the Christians' god is still a Christian world. Secularism is like chastity, a condition defined by what it denies. If atheism has a future, it can only be in a Christian revival; but in fact Christianity and atheism are declining together.

Atheism is a late bloom of a Christian passion for truth. No pagan is ready to sacrifice the pleasure of life for the sake of mere truth. It is artful illusion, not unadorned reality, that they prize. Among the Greeks, the goal of philosophy was happiness or salvation, not truth. The worship of truth is a Christian cult.

The old pagans were right to shudder at the uncouth earnestness of the early Christians. None of the mystery religions in which the ancient world abounded claimed what Christians claimed – that all other faiths were in error. For that very reason, none of their followers could ever become an atheist. When Christians insisted that they alone possessed the truth they condemned the lush profusion of the pagan world with a damning finality.

In a world of many gods, unbelief can never be total. It can only be rejection of one god and acceptance of another, or else – as in Epicurus and his followers – the conviction that the gods do not matter since they have long since ceased to bother about human affairs.

Christianity struck at the root of pagan tolerance of illusion. In claiming that there is only one true faith, it gave truth a supreme value it had not had before. It also made disbelief in the divine possible for the first time. The long-delayed consequence of Christian faith was an idolatry of truth that found its most complete expression in atheism. If we live in a world without gods, we have Christianity to thank for it.

5

HOMER'S VULTURES

Nietzsche's Superman sees mankind falling into an abyss in which nothing has meaning. By a supreme act of will, he delivers man from nihilism. Zarathustra succeeds Jesus as the redeemer of the world.

Nihilism is the idea that human life must be redeemed from meaninglessness. Until Christianity came on the scene, there were no nihilists. In the *Iliad*, Homer sang of the gods provoking men to war so they could enjoy the spectacle of ruin:

> . . . Athene and the lord of the silver bow, Apollo,
> assuming the likeness of birds, of vultures, settled
> aloft the great oak tree of their father, Zeus of the aegis,
> taking their ease and watching these men whose ranks,
>   dense-settled,
> shuddering into a bristle of spears, of shields and of
>   helmets.
> As when the shudder of the west wind suddenly rising
> scatters across the water, and the water darkens
>   beneath it,
> so darkening were settled the ranks of Achaians and
>   Trojans
> in the plain.

Where is nihilism here? Homer's vultures do not redeem human life. There is nothing in it that needs redemption.

6

IN SEARCH OF MORTALITY

The Buddha sought salvation in the extinction of the self; but if there is no self, what is there to be saved?

Nirvana is the end of suffering; but this promises no more than what we all achieve, usually without too much effort, in the course of nature. Death brings to everyone the peace the Buddha promised after lifetimes of striving.

The Buddha sought release from the round of rebirth. E. M. Cioran writes:

> The search for deliverance is justified only if we believe in transmigration, in the indefinite vagabondage of the self, and if we aspire to put an end to it. But for those of us who do not believe in this, what is there to put an end to? To this unique and infinitesimal duration? It is obviously too brief to deserve the exertion of withdrawing from it.

Why do other animals not seek deliverance from suffering? Is it that no one has told them they must live again? Or is it that, without needing to think about it, they know they will not? Cyril Connolly wrote: 'Imagine a cow or a pig which rejected the body for a "noble eightfold way of self-enlightenment". One would feel that the beast had made a false calculation.'

Buddhism is a quest for mortality. The Buddha promised his followers the freedom from sorrow that comes with not having to live again. For those who know themselves to be mortals, what the Buddha sought is always near at hand. Since deliverance is assured, why deny ourselves the pleasure of life?

7

DYING ANIMALS

We think we differ from other animals because we can envision our deaths, when we know no more than they do about what death brings. Everything tells us that it means extinction, but we cannot begin to imagine what that means. The truth is, we do not fear the passing of time because we know death. We fear death because we resist passing time. If other animals do not fear death as we do, it is not because we know something they do not. It is because they are not burdened by time.

We think of suicide as a uniquely human privilege. We are blind to how alike are the ways in which we and other animals do away with ourselves. Until a century or so ago, it was common for people to let themselves be carried off by pneumonia ('the old man's friend') or to step up their daily intake of opiates until they fell asleep for ever. The men and women who did this turned towards death, sometimes consciously, but more often in an instinctual movement no different from that in which a cat seeks a quiet place to see out its end.

As humanity has become more 'moral', it has put such deaths beyond reach. The Greeks and the Romans chose death rather than a worthless life. Today we have made a fetish of choice; but a chosen death is forbidden. Perhaps what distinguishes humans from other animals is that humans have learnt to cling more abjectly to life.

One of the few statements by a European writer that the deaths of humans are no different from those of other animals appears under the name of Bernardo Soares.

> If I carefully consider the life a man leads, I find nothing to distinguish it from the life an animal leads. Both man and animal are hurled unconsciously through things and the world; both have interludes of amusement; both daily follow the same organic itinerary; both think nothing beyond what they think, nor live beyond what they live. A cat wallows in the sun and goes to sleep. Man wallows in life, with all its complexities, and goes to sleep. Neither one escapes the fatal law of being who or what it is.

'Bernardo Soares' was one of many imagined identities assumed by the great Portuguese writer Fernando Pessoa. Some truths cannot be told except as fiction.

8

KRISHNAMURTI'S BURDEN

The Theosophists – an early New Age cult that flourished in many parts of the world in the late nineteenth and early twentieth centuries – groomed Jiddu Krishnamurti as a new messiah, the next in a line of saviours of humanity that included Jesus and Buddha. In early manhood Krishnamurti publicly renounced the role. Ever after, he held that each person had to work out his own salvation. No saviour could relieve us of that burden.

Krishnamurti's teaching has much in common with the mystical traditions he rejected. Mystical philosophies promise an enlightenment that will deliver us from suffering; but the hope they offer is a burden better laid down. Humans cannot leave behind the life they share with other animals. Nor are they wise to try. Anxiety and suffering are as natural to them as serenity and joy. It is when they believe they have left their animal nature behind that humans show the qualities that are theirs alone: obsession, self-deception and perpetual unrest.

From what is known of Krishnamurti's life, it appears to have been a tale of more than ordinary egoism. Like many others, he had secret sexual relationships; but unlike the common run of mankind he was able to use his position as a spiritual teacher to cow those around him into submission. He preached selflessness; but he organised his life to allow him to combine mystical ecstasy with more commonplace consolations. He seems never to have noticed any incongruity in the way he lived.

There is nothing surprising in this. Those who spurn their animal nature do not cease to be human, they merely become caricatures of humanity. Fortunately, the mass of humankind reveres its saints and despises them in equal measure.

9

GURDJIEFF'S 'WORK' AND STANISLAVSKI'S 'METHOD'

The twentieth-century Russian magus G. I. Gurdjieff never tired of repeating that modern humans are machines, and that their mechanicalness comes from the fact that they are not conscious. Did he not see that the more conscious human beings are, the more mechanical they become?

Certainly he perceived that humans in whom consciousness is highly developed cannot help becoming actors. Hence the kinship between Gurdjieff's 'work' and Constantin Stanislavsky's 'method'. Occultists who seek Gurdjieff's inspiration in Sufi or Tibetan teachings should look closer to home. The greatest influence on this latter-day shaman may have been a twentieth-century theory of acting.

Gurdjieff used theatre and dance as devices to assist disciples to gain mastery of their bodily movements and thereby – he claimed – to awake from the common sleep. It is hardly coincidental that his 'work' should have been an influence on some of the most radical developments in theatre. Following Gurdjieff, dramatists such as Peter Brook and Jerzy Grotowski have used theatre as a laboratory in which to explore the nature of human action.

Perhaps training actors was the real aim of Gurdjieff's 'work'. As he said: 'Everyone should try to be an actor. This is a high aim. The aim of every religion, of every knowledge, is to be an actor.' What would a human life be if it was all acting? Gurdjieff's awakened human being could only be an actor in a script written by someone else. Cut off from the unconscious emotions and perceptions that give meaning to the lives of sleeping humans, a fully conscious human being could only be an automaton, controlled not from within but by another human being.

Gurdjieff may genuinely have believed that the more conscious we become, the more creative we can be in our lives. Stanislavsky knew better. 'When he has exhausted all avenues and methods of creativeness an actor reaches a limit beyond which human consciousness cannot extend . . . only nature can perform the miracle without which the text of a role remains lifeless and inert.'

10

THE AERODROME

A poetic image of the view of human possibilities common among Fascists in the thirties is presented in Rex Warner's wartime novel *The Aerodrome*. An exploration of the appeal of Fascism to the progressive mind, it is also a love story.

The action takes place in an aerodrome outside a wretched village, whose inhabitants stumble through lives of sloth and maudlin passion. Whereas the villagers are ruled by habit, the airmen are dedicated to a Nietzschean philosophy, summarised in a speech to them by the Air Vice Marshal:

Your purpose – to escape the bondage of time, to obtain mastery over yourselves, and thus over your environment – must never waver . . . we in this Force are in process of becoming a new and more adequate race of men . . . Science will show you that in our species the period of physical evolution is over. There remains the evolution, or rather the transformation, of consciousness and will, the escape from time, the mastery of the self, a task which has in fact been attempted with some success by individuals at various periods, but which now is to be attempted by all.

The Air Vice Marshal's philosophy demands that airmen cut themselves off from love and family. Yet his own life demonstrates that this is impossible. In a turn of events that is part tragedy and part farce, the narrator discovers that he is the Air Vice Marshal's son. The Air Vice Marshal pleads with him to turn his back on the messy life of the village:

Can you not see . . . what I mean when I urge you to escape from all this, to escape from time and its bondage, to construct around you in your brief existence something that is guided by your own will, not forced upon you by past accidents, something of clarity, independence, and beauty?

But the narrator rejects the life of the Aerodrome for a life of ordinary love of the sort his father despises.

The Air Vice Marshal's philosophy may be a caricature, but it expresses a powerful trend in modern thought. From Francis Bacon to Nietzsche, Enlightenment thinkers have lauded will over the purposeless life of common humanity. Other animals may live without knowing why, but humans can impress a purpose on their lives. They can raise themselves up from the contingent world and rule over it.

There have always been Enlightenment thinkers who do not share this vision. David Hume saw humans as a highly inventive species, but otherwise very like other animals. Through the power of invention they could ease their lot, but they could not overcome it. History was not a tale of progress, but a succession of cycles in which civilisation alternated with barbarism. Hume expected no more than this. Perhaps for that reason, he has had little influence.

The radical right-wing movements of the interwar years were not enemies of 'Western civilisation' so much as its illegitimate offspring. The Fascists and Nazis had nothing but contempt for Enlightenment scepticism and toleration, and many of them scorned Christianity. But – however perversely – Hitler and his followers shared the Enlightenment's faith in human progress, a faith that Christianity had kindled. In embracing the grandiose view of human possibilities represented by the Air Vice Marshal, the interwar Fascists were followers of a Christian heresy. Strange as it may sound, the Aerodrome could not have been built in a land without churches.

11

NIKOLAI FEDOROV, BOLSHEVISM AND THE TECHNOLOGICAL
PURSUIT OF IMMORTALITY

For the nineteenth-century Russian thinker Nikolai Fedorov (1828–1903), nature was the enemy because it condemned the human personality to extinction. The only worthwhile human project was a titanic struggle for immortality. But for Fedorov it was not enough that future generations should have done with death. Only when all the human beings who had ever lived were raised from the dead would the species truly become immortal. The human enterprise was the technological resurrection of the dead.

It seems unbelievable that these fantasies could ever have had a practical influence. Yet Fedorov's thinking was one of the intellectual currents that shaped the Soviet regime. The Bolsheviks believed man to be destined for dominion over nature. More, influenced by Fedorov, they believed that technology could emancipate mankind from the Earth itself. Fedorov's ideas inspired the Russian rocket engineer Konstantin Tsiolkovsky (1857–1935) and through him the first generation of Soviet space explorers. Fedorovian ideas animated the Soviet regime from its beginnings to its very end.

Fedorov's view of humanity as a *chosen species*, destined to conquer the Earth and defeat mortality, is a modern formulation of an ancient faith. Platonism and Christianity have always held that humans do not belong in the natural world.

When they imagined that humanity could rid itself from the limits that surround all other animal species, the thinkers of the Enlightenment merely renewed this ancient error.

Fedorov was undoubtedly extreme, but he was only the most intrepid exponent of a view of things that animated much of the Enlightenment. Henri de Saint-Simon and Auguste Comte looked to a future in which technology would be used to secure dominion over the Earth. This fusion of technological Gnosticism with Enlightenment humanism inspired Karl Marx, who transmitted it to his followers in Russia.

The practical effects of the Marxian-Fedorovian cult of technology were ruinous. Inspired by a materialist philosophy, the Soviet Union inflicted more far-reaching and lasting damage on the material environment than any regime in history. Green earth became desert, and pollution rose to life-threatening levels. No advantage to mankind was gained by the Soviet destruction of nature. Soviet citizens lived no longer than people in other countries – many of them a good deal less.

Resistance to Fedorovian policies was one of the forces that triggered the Soviet collapse. The explosion in the nuclear reactor at Chernobyl galvanised protest all over the country. Much of the opposition to Gorbachev focused on his scheme for redirecting some of Russia's rivers, which would have flooded large parts of Siberia and – as a consequence – altered the world's climate. Mercifully, Gorbachev was toppled, and this grandiose folly never came to pass. Even so, the Soviet legacy to post-communist Russia was a devastated environment – a legacy that its semi-criminal, slash-and-burn capitalism has only made yet more catastrophic.

The cult of technological immortality has not died out. It is alive today in the most advanced capitalist countries. In California there are organisations that offer a technological resurrection to frozen corpses. They promise that cryogenics – the technology of freezing recently living tissue and later warming it back to life – will make us immortal. These cults are proof that – among us, heirs of Christianity and the Enlightenment – eschatology and technology belong together.

It is not that resurrecting the dead will always be a technical impossibility. Perhaps, one way or another, it will someday be feasible. The fatal snag in the promise of cryogenic immortality is not that it exaggerates the powers of technology. It is that the societies in which promises of technological immortality are believed are themselves mortal.

Technological immortalists imagine that the society that exists today will last for ever. In fact, by the time the techniques are available to bring them back to life, the frozen dead will long ago have melted away. War, revolution or economic collapse will have laid waste to the cryonic mausoleums in which they silently await their resurrection.

The technological pursuit of immortality is not a scientific project. It promises what religion has always promised – to give us freedom from fate and chance.

12

ARTIFICIAL PARADISES

In 'Mescal: A New Artificial Paradise', Havelock Ellis wrote of his visions while taking the drug: they 'never resembled familiar objects; they were extremely definite, but yet always novel; they were constantly approaching, and yet constantly eluding, the semblance of known things'.

Eluding the semblance of known things by the use of drugs is one of the perennial avocations of mankind. Paintings from sometime around the end of the last Ice Age discovered in a cave in Pergouset in southwest France show animal figures, probably representing the drug experiences of artists some twelve to fifteen thousand years ago. Shamans have used drugs from time immemorial. In some parts of the world, plants may have first been domesticated for their psychoactive properties. In what has been described by Richard Rudgley as 'a first footstep to agriculture in Australia', the Aborigines harvested and cured various species of tobacco-bearing plants, apparently with the aim of enhancing their mind-altering properties.

There is nothing peculiarly human about the use of drugs. Both in captivity and in the wild, many other animals have been shown to seek out intoxicants. In his book *The Soul of the Ape*, Eugene Marais – himself a morphine addict – showed that wild chacma baboons used intoxicants to disrupt the tedium of ordinary consciousness. In times of plenty when many other fruits were easily available, they went out of their way to eat a rare plumlike fruit, after which they showed all the signs of intoxication. Summarising his findings, which are supported by later research, Marais wrote: 'The habitual use of poisons for the purpose of inducing euphoria – a feeling of mental wellbeing and happiness – is a universal remedy for the pain of consciousness.'

It is a result that applies as much to humans as to baboons. Consciousness and the attempt to escape it go together. Drug use is a primordial animal activity. Among humans, it is immemorial and nearly universal. What then accounts for the 'war on drugs'?

Prohibiting drugs makes the trade in them fabulously profitable. It breeds crime and greatly enlarges the prison population. Despite this, there is a worldwide drug pandemic. Prohibiting drugs has failed. Why then will no contemporary government legalise them? Some say organised crime and the law are linked in a symbiosis that blocks radical reform. There may be some truth in this, but the real explanation lies elsewhere.

The most pitiless warriors against drugs have always been militant progressives. In China, the most savage attack on drug use occurred when the country was convulsed by a modern western doctrine of universal emancipation – Maoism. It is no accident that the crusade against drugs is led today by a country wedded to the pursuit of happiness – the United States. For the corollary of that improbable quest is a puritan war on pleasure.

Drug use is a tacit admission of a forbidden truth. For most people happiness is beyond reach. Fulfilment is found not in daily life but in escaping from it. Since happiness is un-available, the mass of mankind seeks pleasure.

Religious cultures could admit that earthly life was hard, for they promised another in which all tears would be wiped away. Their humanist successors affirm something still more incredible – that in future, even the near future, everyone can be happy. Societies founded on a faith in progress cannot admit the normal unhappiness of human life. As a result, they are bound to wage war on those who seek an artificial happiness in drugs.

13

GNOSTICISM AND THE CYBERNAUTS

The central character in William Gibson's novel *Neuromancer* is a cybernaut who has lost the freedom to roam the virtual world. Punished for cheating by his former employers, he is compelled to pass his days in his mortal shell. He sees his return to earthly life as confinement: 'For Case, who'd lived for the bodiless exultation of cyberspace, it was the Fall. . . . The body was meat. Case fell into the prison of his own flesh.'

Today's cybernauts are unknowing Gnostics. The flight from the prison of the flesh is the essence of the Gnostic heresy that, despite incessant persecution, persisted in Christendom for centuries, and which survives to this day in the Mandean community in Syria. For Gnostics, the

Earth is a prison of souls, ruled – perhaps created – not by God but by a demiurge, an evil spirit which enticed humans into the captivity of the flesh by showing them the beauty of the world. A twentieth-century Gnostic, C. G. Jung, stated the central Gnostic myth in precisely these terms. He speaks of

> ... that idea of the Gnosis, the *nous*, that beholds his own face in the ocean: he sees the beauty of the earth and ... he is caught, entangled in the problems of the world. Had he remained the *nous* or *pneuma*, he would have kept on the wing, would have been like the image of God that was floating over the waters and never touching them; but he did touch them and that was the beginning of human life, the beginning of the world with all its suffering and beauty, its heavens and hells.

Jesus promised the resurrection of the body, not an afterlife as a disembodied consciousness. Despite this, the followers of Jesus have always disparaged the flesh. Their belief that humans are marked off from the rest of creation by having an immortal soul has led them to disown the fate they share with other animals. They cannot reconcile their attachment to the body with their hope of immortality. When the two come into conflict it is always the flesh that is left behind.

The cult of cyberspace continues the Gnostic flight from the body. Cyberspace offers a promise of eternity that is more radical than what Gibson calls 'the sham immortality of cryo-genics'. The Extropians are a contemporary cult, whose members aim to shed their mortal flesh. Citing Nietzsche's dictum 'Man is something to be overcome', the founder of the cult asks, 'Why seek to become posthuman? . . . Certainly, we can achieve much while remaining human. Yet we can attain higher peaks by applying our intelligence, determination and optimism to break out of the human chrysalis. . . . Our bodies restrain our capacities.'

Once the frail and wasting body is cast off, the Extropians believe, the mind can live for ever. These cybernauts seek to make the thin trickle of consciousness – our shallowest fleeting sensation – everlasting. But we are not embrained phantoms encased in mortal flesh. Being embodied is our nature as earth-born creatures.

Our flesh is easily worn out; but in being so clearly subject to time and accident it reminds us of what we truly are. Our essence lies in what is most accidental about us – the time and place of our birth, our habits of speech and movement, the flaws and quirks of our bodies.

Cybernauts who seek immortality in the ether are ready to disown their bodies for the sake of a deathless existence in the ether. Perhaps someday they will achieve what they crave, but it will be at the price of losing their animal souls.

14

INSIDE THE PHANTOMAT

Computers are now largely invisible. They are embedded everywhere – in walls, tables, chairs, desks, clothing, jewellery, and bodies. People routinely use three-dimensional displays built into their glasses. . . . These 'direct eye' displays create highly realistic, virtual visual environments overlaying the 'real' environment.

Ray Kurzweil

In this anticipation of daily life in 2019, virtual worlds will become ubiquitous. By bracketing 'reality', Kurzweil – one of the pioneers of computer science – points to a possibility that has long intrigued metaphysicians: all reality is virtual. The world disclosed in ordinary perception is a makeshift of habit and convention. Virtual worlds disrupt this consensual hallucination, but in doing so they leave us without a test for a reality that is independent of ourselves.

The disorienting effects of virtual reality have been explored by a number of writers and filmmakers but the first anticipation of its potential rewards and risks occurs in Stanislaw Lem's *Summa Technologiae*, written in 1964. Lem envisages a 'phantomatic generator', which enables users to enter into simulated worlds:

What can the subject experience in the link-up to the phantomatic generator? Everything. He can scale

mountain cliffs or walk without a space suit or oxygen
mask on the surface of the moon; in clanking armour
he can lead a faithful posse to a conquest of medieval
fortifications; he can explore the North Pole. He can
be adulated by crowds as a winner of the Marathon,
accept the Nobel Prize from the hands of the Swedish
king as the greatest poet of all times, indulge in the
requited love of Madame Pompadour, duel with Jason,
revenge Othello, or fall under the daggers of Mafia
hitmen . . . he can die, be resurrected, and then do it
again, many, many times over.

Lem's phantomat is the endpoint in a new technology of virtual reality; but humans have always sought relief from their
lives. Many of their oldest institutions are tributes to the need
for make-believe. As Lem writes:

Phantomatics appears to be a sort of pinnacle towards
which sundry forms and technologies of entertainment
converge. There are already houses of illusion, ghost
houses, funhouses – Disneyland is in fact one big primitive pseudophantomat. Apart from these variations,
permitted by law, there are illicit ones (this is the situation
in Jean Genet's *Balcony*, where the site of pseudophan-
tomatization is a brothel). Phantomatics has a certain
potential to become an art. . . . This could therefore lead
it to split into artistically valuable product and mediocre
kitsch, as with movies or various types of art. The
menace of phantomatics is, however, incomparably

greater than that represented by debased cinema. . . . For, due to its specificity, phantomatics offers the kind of experience which, in its intimacy, is equalled only in a dream.

Lem could have traced his phantomat farther back. Virtual reality is a technological simulation of techniques of lucid dreaming practised by shamans for millennia. Using fasting, music, dance and psychotropic plants, the shaman leaves the everyday world to enter another, returning to find ordinary reality transformed. Like virtual reality technology, shamanistic techniques disrupt the consensual hallucination of everyday life. But with this crucial difference: the shamans know that neither the ordinary world nor the alternate worlds they explore in trance are of their own making.

The phantomat's power comes from the immaculate realism of its illusions. Inside it, we can have only the experiences we want to have. We can escape not only our personal limitations but also those that go with being human. We can swim and climb despite the fact that we lack the ability to do so; we can fly like a bird and live in different epochs in the same lifetime. We seem to escape the limits of our everyday world. Our lives are knotted through with irretrievable acts and unalterable events; but in the phantomat this one and only life of ours is only one of many we can live, an iteration in an unending series in which we can be born, die and be reborn again and again.

What is lost in the phantomat is not the one undying reality that metaphysicians seek in vain. It is the hold on our lives we gain when we know we are mortal. We may believe – as Christians say they do – that this life is a prelude to life everlasting; we may agree with Epicurus that after death we are nothing, so death is nothing to us; or we may affirm with Chuang-Tzu that dying is only waking from a dream, perhaps to another. Whatever we believe, death marks the limit of the only life we know. The phantomat enables us to live, die and be born again at will. By glazing over the fact of mortality, it leaves us with no check on our wishes. Our experiences are confections of our desires, and no longer connect us with anything else: 'Phantomatics means the creation of a situation in which there are no exits from the created fiction to the real world.'

Lem's prescience regarding virtual reality technology is extraordinary; but the risk of all-encompassing unreality to which he points is itself unreal. The idea that we may be on the way to contriving a fiction from which there is no exit endows technology with a power it can never possess. The phantomat is vastly superior to any virtual reality machine we have yet devised. Even so, it can no more enable us to escape fate and chance than the cryogenic vats that promise everlasting life to frozen corpses.

No technology can create a world that matches human desires. Lucid dreaming is a dangerous sport; those who practise it must expect to encounter things they could not have imagined. Whether they allow the shaman to delve into the unconscious or enable him to perceive realities unknown to the rest of us, the worlds he explores are no mere fabrications. They are journeys into unknown lands, stranger than those we know through ordinary perception, but like them in their hidden limits and sudden surprises.

Lem envisaged his phantomat as a generator of perfect illusions, but any actual machine will be prone to accident and decay. Sooner or later, errors will creep into the program its designers have written for it, and the virtual worlds it conjures up will come to resemble the actual world it was meant to transcend. At that point, we will find ourselves once again in a world we have not made. We have dreamt of machines that can deliver us from ourselves; but the dream worlds they make for us contain rifts and gaps that return us to mortal life.

15

THE MIRROR OF SOLITUDE

E. O. Wilson has written: '. . . the next century will see the closing of the Cenozoic Era (the Age of Mammals) and a new one characterized not by new life forms but by biological impoverishment. It might be appropriately called the "Eremozoic Era", the Age of Loneliness.'

Humanity could soon find itself alone, in an empty world. Humans co-opt over 40 per cent of the Earth's living tissue. If, over the next few decades, human numbers increase by half again, well over half the world's organic matter will be given over to humans. Very likely this nightmare will never come to pass. The prosthetic world that humans are creating for themselves will be destroyed, long before it is completed, by the side effects of human activity – war, pollution or disease.

If the present wave of mass extinctions is followed by an Era of Solitude, it will surely be full of mystics. A destitute world will be the site of a revival of piety. Like prayerful astronauts, its inhabitants will look to the heavens for sustenance – and they will not be disappointed. What could be more natural for a species that has exterminated its animal kin than to look into a mirror and find that it is not alone?

Mystics imagine that by seeking out empty places they can open themselves to something other than themselves. Nearly always they do the opposite. They carry the trash and litter of humanity wherever they go.

Mystics talk of finding sermons in stones. For seekers after inhuman truth there could be no worse nightmare. It is only because nature cares nothing for us that it can release us from human cares. Fernando Pessoa writes:

> Only if you don't know what flowers, stones, and
> rivers are
> Can you talk about their feelings.
> To talk about the soul of flowers, stones, and rivers,
> Is to talk about yourself, about your delusions.
> Thank God stones are just stones,
> And rivers just rivers,
> And flowers just flowers.

Anyone who truly wants to escape human solipsism should not seek out empty places. Instead of fleeing to the desert, where they will be thrown back into their own thoughts, they will do better to seek the company of other animals. A zoo is a better window from which to look out of the human world than a monastery.

16

THE COAST OPPOSITE HUMANITY

Nearly all philosophies, most religions and much of science testify to a desperate, unwearying concern with the salvation of mankind. If we turn from solipsism, we will be less concerned with the fate of the human animal. Health and sanity do not lie in an introverted love of human things, but in turning to what Robinson Jeffers in his poem 'Meditation on Saviors' calls 'the coast opposite humanity'.

Homo rapiens is only one of very many species, and not obviously worth preserving. Later or sooner, it will become extinct. When it is gone the Earth will recover. Long after the last traces of the human animal have disappeared, many of the species it is bent on destroying will still be around, along with others that have yet to spring up. The Earth will forget mankind. The play of life will go on.

5
NON-PROGRESS

Progress celebrates Pyrrhic victories over nature.

KARL KRAUS

1

DE QUINCEY'S TOOTHACHE

In the early nineteenth century, Thomas de Quincey wrote that a quarter of human misery was toothache. He may well have been right. Anaesthetic dentistry is an unmixed blessing. So are clean water and flush toilets. Progress is a fact. Even so, faith in progress is a superstition.

Science enables humans to satisfy their needs. It does nothing to change them. They are no different today from what they have always been. There is progress in knowledge, but not in ethics. This is the verdict both of science and history, and the view of every one of the world's religions.

The growth of knowledge is real and – barring a world-wide catastrophe – it is now irreversible. Improvements in government and society are no less real, but they are temporary. Not only can they be lost, they are sure to be. History is not progress or decline, but recurring gain and loss. The advance of knowledge deludes us into thinking we are different from other animals, but our history shows that we are not.

2

THE WHEEL

We think of the Stone Age as an era of poverty and the Neolithic as a great leap forward. In fact the move from hunter-gathering to farming brought no overall gain in human well-being or freedom. It enabled larger numbers to live poorer lives. Almost certainly, Paleolithic humanity was better off.

The turn to farming was not a clear-cut event. Intensive plant gathering may have begun some twenty thousand years ago, cultivation of the land around fifteen thousand years ago. In some parts of the world, it seems to have followed climate change. In the Middle East, rising sea levels at the end of the Ice Age seem to have driven hunter-gatherers into the uplands where they turned to agriculture to survive.

In other areas, the hunter-gatherers destroyed their environment themselves. Only after the first Polynesian settlers had wiped out moas and ravaged the seal population of New Zealand did they turn to more intensive methods of food production. By exterminating the animals on which they depended, these hunter-gatherers condemned their own way of life to extinction.

There was never a Golden Age of harmony with the Earth. Most hunter-gatherers were fully as rapacious as later humans. But they were few, and they lived better than most who came after them.

The move from hunter-gathering to farming has often been seen as a change like the Industrial Revolution of modern times. If this is so, it is because both increased the powers of humans without enhancing their freedom. Hunter-gatherers normally have enough for their needs; they do not have to work to accumulate more. In the eyes of those for whom wealth means having an abundance of objects, the hunter-gathering life must look like poverty. From another angle it can be seen as freedom: 'We are inclined to think of hunter-gatherers as *poor* because they don't have anything; perhaps better to think of them for that reason as *free*,' writes Marshall Sahlins.

The shift from hunter-gathering to farming is conventionally viewed as a move from a nomadic to a settled life. In reality it was almost the opposite. Hunter-gatherers are highly mobile. But their life does not require continuous movement into new territory. Their survival depends on knowing a local milieu down to its last details. Farming multiplies human numbers. It thereby compels farmers to expand the land they work. Farming and the search for new lands go together. As Hugh Brody writes: '. . . it is the agriculturalists, with their commitment to specific farms and large numbers of children, who are forced to keep moving, resettling, colonising new lands. . . . As a system, over time, it is farming, not hunting, that generates "nomadism".'

The move from hunter-gathering to farming harmed health and life expectancy. Even today, the hunter-gatherers of the Arctic and the Kalahari have better diets than poor people in rich countries – and much better than those of many people in so-called developing countries. More of the world's population is chronically undernourished today than in the Old Stone Age.

The shift from hunter-gathering to farming was not only bad for health. It greatly increased the burden of work. The hunter-gatherers of the Old Stone Age may not have lived as long as we do, but they had a more leisurely existence than most people today. Farming increased the power of humans over the Earth. At the same time it impoverished those who turned to it.

The freedom of hunter-gatherers was bounded by restraint. Infanticide, geronticide and sexual abstinence limited their numbers. Once again, these practices can be seen as consequences of their poverty; but they are just as well viewed as ways of maintaining their freedom.

Hunter-gatherers did not take to farming because it gave them a better life. Very probably they had no choice. Whether as a result of climate change, or a slow build-up in population, or because wildlife had declined through over-hunting, hunter-gathering communities found themselves impelled to increase food production.

Hunter-gatherers who took up farming outbred those who did not. Farmers drove the remaining hunter-gatherers into less hospitable territory, or simply killed them off. The remainder were driven to the edge of the world, marginal lands such as the Kalahari where they linger today.

The shift to farming did not have a single source. But wherever it happened it was both an effect and a cause of growth in human numbers. Farming became indispensable because of the larger population it made possible. From that point onwards there was no turning back.

History is a treadmill turned by rising human numbers. Today GM crops are being marketed as the only means of avoiding mass starvation. They are unlikely to improve the lives of peasant farmers; but they may well enable them to survive in greater numbers. Genetic crop modification is another turn in a wheel that has been in motion since the passing of hunter-gathering.

3

AN IRONY OF HISTORY

One of the pioneers of robotics has written: 'In the next century inexpensive but capable robots will displace human labour so broadly that the average workday would have to plummet to practically zero to keep everyone employed.'

Hans Moravec's vision of the future may be closer than we think. New technologies are rapidly displacing human labour. The 'underclass' of the permanently unemployed is partly the result of poor education and misguided economic policies. Yet it is time that increasing numbers are becoming economically redundant. It is no longer unthinkable that within a few generations the majority of the population will have little or no role in the production process.

The chief effect of the Industrial Revolution was to engender the working class. It did this not so much by forcing a shift from the country to towns as by enabling a massive growth in population. At the beginning of the twenty-first century, a new phase of the Industrial Revolution is under way that promises to make much of that population superfluous.

Today the Industrial Revolution that began in the towns of northern England has become worldwide. The result is the global expansion in population we are presently witnessing. At the same time, new technologies are steadily stripping away the functions of the labour force that the Industrial Revolution has created.

An economy whose core tasks are done by machines will value human labour only in so far as it cannot be replaced. Moravec writes: 'Many trends in industrialized societies lead to a future where humans are supported by machines, as our ancestors were by wildlife.' That, according to Jeremy Rifkin, does not mean mass unemployment. Rather, we are approaching a time when, in Moravec's words, 'almost all humans work to amuse other humans'.

In rich countries, that time has already arrived. The old industries have been exported to the developing world. At home, new occupations have evolved, replacing those of the industrial era. Many of them satisfy needs that in the past were repressed or disguised. A thriving economy of psychotherapists, designer religions and spiritual boutiques has sprung up. Beyond that, there is an enormous grey economy of illegal industries supplying drugs and sex. The function of this new economy, legal and illegal, is to entertain and distract a population which – though it is busier than ever before – secretly suspects that it is useless.

Industrialisation created the working class. Now it has made the working class obsolete. Unless it is cut short by ecological collapse, it will eventually do the same to nearly everyone.

4

THE DISCREET POVERTY OF THE FORMER MIDDLE CLASSES

Bourgeois life was based on the institution of the *career* – a lifelong pathway through working life. Today professions and occupations are disappearing. Soon they will be as remote and archaic as the ranks and estates of medieval times.

Our only real religion is a shallow faith in the future; and yet we have no idea what the future will bring. None but the incorrigibly feckless any longer believe in taking the long view. Saving is gambling, careers and pensions are high-level punts. The few who are seriously rich hedge their bets. The proles – the rest of us – live from day to day.

In Europe and Japan, bourgeois life lingers on. In Britain and America it has become the stuff of theme parks. The middle class is a luxury capitalism can no longer afford.

5

THE END OF EQUALITY

The welfare state was a by-product of the Second World War. The National Health Service began in the Blitz, full employment in conscription. Postwar egalitarianism was an after-effect of mass mobilisation in war.

Look back to the nineteenth century, to the time between the end of the Napoleonic Wars and the outbreak of the

First World War. That great era of peace in Europe was also a period of great inequality. The majority of the population lived from hand to mouth, and only the very rich were safe from sudden poverty. Today, nearly everyone is much better off. Yet the rackety existence of the majority is as far removed from the security enjoyed by the truly wealthy as it was in Victorian times.

In affluent, high-tech economies, the masses are superfluous – even as cannon fodder. Wars are no longer fought by conscript armies but by computers – and, in the collapsed states that litter much of the world, by the ragged irregular armies of the poor. With this mutation of war, the pressure to maintain social cohesion is relaxed. The wealthy can pass their lives without contact with the rest of society. So long as they do not pose a threat to the rich, the poor can be left to their own devices.

Social democracy has been replaced by an oligarchy of the rich as part of the price of peace.

6

A BILLION BALCONIES FACING THE SUN

The days when the economy was dominated by agriculture are long gone. Those of industry are nearly over. Economic life is no longer geared chiefly to production. To what then is it geared? To distraction.

Contemporary capitalism is prodigiously productive, but

the imperative that drives it is not productivity. It is to keep boredom at bay. Where affluence is the rule the chief threat is the loss of desire. With wants so quickly sated, the economy soon comes to depend on the manufacture of ever more exotic needs.

What is new is not that prosperity depends on stimulating demand. It is that it cannot continue without inventing new vices. The economy is driven by an imperative of perpetual novelty, and its health has come to depend on the manufacture of transgression. The spectre that haunts it is glut – not of physical goods only, but of experiences that have palled. New experiences become obsolete even more quickly than do physical commodities.

Adherents of 'traditional values' rail against contemporary licence. They have chosen to forget what every traditional society understood – that virtue cannot do without the solace of vice. More to the point, they are blind to the economic necessity of new vices. Designer drugs and designer sex are prototypical twenty-first-century commodities. This is not because, in the words of J. H. Prynne's poem:

Music

travel, habit and silence are all *money*

– though that is what they are. It is because new vices are prophylactics against the loss of desire. Ecstasy, Viagra, the S-and-M parlours of New York and Frankfurt are not just aids to pleasure. They are antidotes to boredom. In a time when satiety is a threat to prosperity, pleasures that were forbidden in the past have become the staples of the new economy.

Perhaps we are lucky to be spared the rigours of idleness. In his novel *Cocaine Nights*, J. G. Ballard presents the Club Nautico, an exclusive enclave for rich British retirees in the Spanish resort of Estrella del Mar:

> The memory-erasing white architecture; the enforced leisure that fossilised the nervous system; the almost Africanised aspect, but a North Africa invented by someone who had never visited the Maghreb; the apparent absence of any social structure; the timelessness of a world beyond boredom, with no past, no future and a diminishing present. Perhaps this is what a leisure-dominated future would resemble? Nothing would ever happen in this affectless realm, where entropic drift calmed the surfaces of a thousand swimming pools.

In order to stave off psychic entropy, society resorts to unorthodox therapies:

> Our governments are preparing for a future without work. . . . People will work, or rather some people will work, but only for a decade of their lives. They will retire in their late thirties, with fifty years of idleness in front of them. . . . A billion balconies facing the sun.

Only the thrill of the forbidden can lighten the burden of a life of leisure:

Only one thing is left which can rouse people. . . .
Crime, and transgressive behaviour – by which I mean
all activities that aren't necessarily illegal, but provoke us
and tap our need for strong emotion, quicken the nervous system and jump the synapses deadened by leisure
and inaction.

Ballard's prospect of 'a billion balconies facing the sun' has
proved to be deceptive. In the twenty-first century the rich
work harder than they have ever done. Even the poor are
spared the perils that go with having too much time on their
hands. But the problems of social control in an overworked
society are not so different from those in a world of enforced
leisure. In a later novel, *Super-Cannes*, Ballard portrays the
model business community of Eden-Olympia, where the
accidie of burnt-out executives is treated with a regime of
'carefully metered violence, a microdose of madness like the
minute traces of strychnine in a nerve tonic'. The remedy for
senseless work is a therapeutic regime of senseless violence –
carefully choreographed street fights, muggings, burglaries,
rapes and other, even more deviant recreations.

The rationale of this regime is explained by the resident
psychologist who orchestrates these experiments in controlled
psychopathy: 'The consumer society hungers for the deviant
and the unexpected. What else can drive the bizarre shifts in
the entertainment landscape that will keep us buying?'

Today the doses of madness that keep us sane are supplied
by new technologies. Anyone online has a limitless supply of
virtual sex and violence. But what will happen when we run

out of new vices? How will satiety and idleness be staved off when designer sex, drugs and violence no longer sell? At that point, we may be sure, morality will come back into fashion. We may not be far from a time when 'morality' is marketed as a new brand of transgression.

7

TWENTIETH-CENTURY ANTI-CAPITALISTS, THE PHALANSTERY AND THE MEDIEVAL BRETHREN OF THE FREE SPIRIT

A generation ago, an obscure revolutionary group calling themselves Situationists inspired anti-capitalist riots that shook the capitals of Europe.

The Situationists were a small and exclusive sect, which claimed to possess a unique perspective on the world. In reality their view of things was a *mélange* of nineteenth-century revolutionary theories and twentieth-century vanguardist art. They took many of their ideas from anarchism and Marxism, Surrealism and Dada. But their most audacious borrowings were from a late-medieval sodality of mystical anarchists, the Brethren of the Free Spirit.

The Situationists were heirs to a fraternity of adepts that extended across much of medieval Europe, and which – despite unceasing persecution – persisted as an identifiable tradition for over five hundred years. The Situationists' dream was the same as that of this millenarian cult – a society in which all things were held in common and no one was forced to work. In the early sixties, they enlivened student protests in Strasbourg with quotes from the medieval revolutionaries. During the events of 1968, they scrawled similar graffiti on the walls of Paris. Among the most memorable of these was *Never work!*

Like the Brethren of the Free Spirit, the Situationists dreamt of a world in which labour had given way to play. As one of them, Raoul Vaneigem, wrote: 'Taking into account my time and the objective help it gives me, have I said any more in the twentieth century than the Brethren of the Free Spirit declared in the thirteenth?' Vaneigem was right to see modern revolutionary movements as heirs to the mystical anarchist cults of the Middle Ages. In both cases, their goals came not from science, but from the eschatological fantasies of religion.

Marx scorned utopianism as unscientific. But if 'scientific socialism' resembles any science, it is alchemy. Along with other Enlightenment thinkers, Marx believed that technology could transmute the base metal of human nature into gold. In the communist society of the future, there was to be no limit on the growth of production or the expansion of human numbers. With the abolition of scarcity, private property, the family, the state and the division of labour would disappear.

Marx imagined the end of scarcity would bring the end of history. He could not bring himself to see that a world without scarcity had already been achieved – in the prehistoric societies that he and Engels lumped together as 'primitive communism'. Hunter-gatherers were less burdened by labour than the majority of mankind at any later stage, but their sparse communities were completely dependent on the Earth's bounty. Natural catastrophe could wipe them out at any time.

Marx could not accept the constraint that was the price of the hunter-gatherers' freedom. Instead, animated by the faith that humans are destined to master the Earth, he insisted that freedom from labour could be achieved without any restraints on their desires. This was only the Brethren of the Free Spirit's apocalyptic fantasy returning as an Enlightenment utopia.

More even than Marx, the Situationists dreamt of a world without, in Vaneigem's words, 'the time of work, progress and output, production, consumption and programming'. Labour would be abolished, and humanity would be at liberty to indulge its whims. This dream owes a great deal to Marx, but it resembles still more the fantasies of Charles François Fourier, the early-nineteenth-century French utopian. Fourier proposed that in future humanity should live in monasterylike institutions, *phalanstères*, in which free love is practised and no one is compelled to work. In Fourier's utopia, *homo ludens* rules.

The Situationists' utopia is an updated version of Fourier's but, in a lapse of mind they seem never to have noticed, the administration of this workless society is handed over to workers' councils. These are not meant to be organs of government, for – we are assured – none will be needed. Going even further than Fourier, who had proposed that dirty work be done by children, the Situationists declared that automation would make physical labour unnecessary. Without scarcity or work, there would be no need for conflict. As in Marx's utopian vision, the state would wither away.

As far as the future was concerned, the Situationists were unshakeably confident. About the present, they were darkly pessimistic. A new form of domination had been perfected, they maintained, in which every act of apparent dissent actually takes place in a worldwide spectacle. Life had been turned into a show, which even those who staged the play could not escape. The most radical movements of revolt quickly became part of the act.

In a familiar irony, that is exactly what happened to the Situationists. Their ideas soon reappeared as the cleverly marketed nihilism of punk rock bands. Despite their protestations, the Situationists soon became just one more commodity in the cultural supermarket.

The revolution of which they dreamt was nowhere in sight. Yet they retained an unruffled certainty. Their most gifted thinker, Guy Debord, insisted: 'a change-over is imminent and ineluctable . . . like lightning, which we know only when it strikes'. In the purest millenarian tradition, Debord believed that dark forces ruled the world – and that their power was about to vanish overnight. His apocalyptic serenity did not last. Perhaps the evident absurdity of his hopes of a worldwide proletarian revolution against consumer culture finally sank in. Or it may be that more personal factors were at work. In 1984 Debord's publisher was murdered, and in 1991 his widow tried to sell the company. Debord was at a loss. In a memorably farcical episode, the uncompromising refuser of the spectacle advertised for a literary agent in the

Times Literary Supplement. It is not known if there were any replies. In any event, Debord signed with a new publisher, Gallimard, and his work gained wider currency; but his mood did not improve. A lifelong drinking habit induced deepening depression. In 1994, at the age of sixty-two, he shot himself.

The Situationists and the Brethren of the Free Spirit are separated by centuries, but their view of human possibilities is the same. Humans are gods stranded in a world of darkness. Their labours are not the natural consequence of their inordinate wants. They are the curse of a demiurge. All that needs to be done to free humanity from labour is to throw off this evil power. This mystical vision is the Situationists' true inspiration, and that of anyone who has ever dreamt of a world in which humans can live without restraint.

8

MESMERISM AND THE NEW ECONOMY

Markets have always been partly figments, but today they are more so than ever before. New technologies do more than transmit information. They change behaviour by propagating moods. Not only does everyone receive news faster than before, the mood it creates is far more swiftly contagious. The Internet confirms what has long been known – the world is ruled by the power of suggestion.

In late-eighteenth- and early-nineteenth-century Austria, Anton Mesmer showed that hypnotic suggestion can have a profound effect on human behaviour. Ridiculed in his life-time, Mesmer was remembered through the popular name for hypnosis – mesmerism. Sixty years later, Jean Charcot showed the connection between hypnosis and hysteria, and became one of the founders of psychiatry.

Financial markets are moved by contagion and hysteria. New communications technologies magnify suggestibility. Mesmer and Charcot are better guides to the new economy than Hayek or Keynes.

9

A THEORY OF CONSCIOUSNESS

In evolutionary prehistory, consciousness emerged as a side effect of language. Today it is a by-product of the media.

10

MEMORIES IN STONES

Conservationists lament the passing of wild places, but cities too are endangered ecosystems. Since Neolithic times, when they first began to emerge in places such as Çatal Hüyük in contemporary Anatolia, cities have been places where humans re-enact the rituals of hunter-gatherers. Humans are ill suited to the incessant labour and recurrent migration that go with farming. Cities were created from the yearning for a settled existence.

Hunter-gatherers must know their local environment intimately. They need to move freely on the land so they can track its changes; but they are not bound to move into new territory, as farmers must when they have exhausted the soil. The lives of hunter-gatherers circle around a place they never leave, or cease to explore.

All cities were once new; but it is ancient cities that best meet the need for a settled existence. Iain Sinclair believes old cities bear the psychic traces of the generations that have passed through them:

> The churches are only one system of energies, or unit of connection, within the city. There are also the old hospitals, the Inns of Court, the markets, the prisons, the religious houses. . . . Each church is an enclosure of force, a sight-block, a raised place with an unacknowledged influence on events.

Old cities are descendants in a line that goes back to the Labyrinth at Knossos in Bronze Age Crete.

In cities, persons are shadows cast by places, and no generation lasts as long as a street. In the post-urban sprawls that are replacing cities, streets come and go as quickly as the people who pass through them. As cities are deconstructed into sites for traffic, the settled life they once contained is fading from memory.

11

THE MYTH OF MODERNISATION

We are all modernisers today. We have no idea what being modern means. But we are sure that it guarantees us a future.

For nineteenth-century Positivists, modernity meant a new version of medievalism – a hierarchical technocracy in which science replaced religion; for Marx and the Webbs it meant an economy without markets or private property; for Francis Fukuyama, it meant a worldwide free market and universal liberal democracy. Each of these quite different visions has been seen as the very essence of modernity. All have proved to be fantasies.

We think of modernity as an idea in the social sciences, when actually it is the last hiding place of 'morality'. Believers in modernity are convinced that – natural disasters apart – history is on the side of Enlightenment values. After all, that is what being modern means, is it not?

In fact, there are many ways of being modern, and many of failing to be. It is not for nothing that a number of the Expressionists were among Nazism's early supporters, or that Oswald Mosley gave press interviews seated behind a black steel Futurist desk. The Nazis were committed to a revolutionary transformation of European life. For them, becoming modern meant racial conquest and genocide. Any society that systematically uses science and technology to achieve its goals is modern. Death camps are as modern as laser surgery.

A feature of the idea of modernity is that the future of mankind is always taken to be secular. Nothing in history has ever supported this strange notion. Secularisation has occurred in a few European countries such as England, Sweden and Italy. There is no sign of it in the United States. Among Islamic countries, only Turkey has a well-entrenched secular state; in most others fundamentalism is on the rise. In India, Hindu nationalism has eroded the secular state. In China and Japan, where the Judaeo-Christian and Islamic idea of religion has never been accepted, secularism is practically meaningless. Despite these facts, twenty-first-century modernisers talk in the dated accents of Marx and the Positivists, nineteenth-century Europeans who mistook their parochial hopes for universal historical laws.

Theories of modernisation are cod-scientific projections of Enlightenment values. They tell us nothing about the future. But they do help us to understand the present. They show the lingering power of the Christian faith that history is a moral drama, a tale of progress or redemption, in which – despite everything we know of it – morality rules the world.

12

AL QAEDA

The men who hijacked civilian planes and used them as weapons to attack New York and Washington, D.C., in September 2001 did more than demonstrate the vulnerability of the world's strongest power. They destroyed an entire view of the world.

Everyone believed the world was becoming steadily more secular. Yet on 11 September war and religion were as deeply intertwined as ever they had been in human history. The terrorists were foot soldiers in a new war of religion.

Everyone took for granted that the world was at peace. States everywhere were linked up in a worldwide network of free markets. Even the biggest of them – China – was signing up to global capitalism. Free trade had made war obsolete. But the World Trade Center was razed to the ground in a new kind of war.

Everyone assumed that war meant conflict between states. Despite the evidence of twentieth-century guerrilla warfare, the idea persisted that if war were to come again – and few people were ready to admit that it could – it would be an affair of armies and governments. But the network that concerted the attacks on Washington, D.C., and New York was more like a postmodern corporation than an old-fashioned army. Al Qaeda took orders from no state, it exploited the weakness of states. A by-product of 'globalisation', it successfully privatised terror and projected it worldwide.

Everyone accepted that with globalisation 'modern values' were in the ascendant. But if globalisation means anything, it is the chaotic drift of new technologies. If it has any overall effect, it is not to spread 'modern values' but to consume them.

In that it makes extensive use of the Internet, Al Qaeda is certainly 'modern'; but it uses the Internet to repudiate

Western modernity. In so far as it draws on the support of clan networks, Al Qaeda embodies 'premodern' social structures; but its refusal of 'modern values' expresses an act of will rather than any established tradition or authority. In that, Al Qaeda is peculiarly 'modern'.

A 'postmodern' organisation serving 'premodern' values, Al Qaeda has planted a question mark over the very idea of what it means to be modern.

13

THE LESSON OF JAPAN

To say that humans can never master technology does not mean they have no control over it. It means the extent of their control does not depend on their will.

Several countries have tried to shut out new technology. For a time China gave up ocean-going ships. But the Japanese case is unique in that it involved the deliberate and sustained rejection of a key modern technology. Between 1543 and 1879 Japan gave up the gun and reverted to the sword. From having more guns than any other country in the world it succeeded in eliminating them almost entirely.

At the time it embarked on its unique experiment, Japan had several rare advantages. It was isolated and could hope to remain so. It was a highly cohesive society. It had a subtle and far-seeing ruling class, which included a strategically placed group – the samurai – that stood to gain by a policy of reverting to the sword. Taken together, these conditions enabled Japan to reject guns for several centuries.

During its time of isolation Japan was not stagnant. While shutting out guns, it produced many technical innovations of its own. A new kind of two-bladed plough, a spiked-wheel potato planter and a new kind of weeding machine were developed during the time of Japan's isolation. In many ways, the country's development was equal, or superior, to that of Western countries at the time: in cities, public health was better, and its postal service was more developed. There was technical innovation in Japan during the centuries in which it isolated itself, but it was slow and piecemeal, serving a traditional way of life. Noel Perrin writes:

> There were armoured knights striding around Tokyo and Kagoshima when the Continental Congress was meeting in Philadelphia – but a letter, or a shipment of lacquer seedlings, travelled many times faster between those two cities than mail did between Philadelphia and Savannah.

Japan's rulers were able to shut out the modern technologies that threatened its peace because it had the option of isolation. When Commodore Perry arrived with his black ships in 1853, Japan's rulers knew it had to switch course. By the first decade of the twentieth century it had a modern navy, which destroyed the Russian Imperial Fleet at the Battle of Tsushima – the first time a modern European power was defeated in war by an Asian people.

Any country that renounces technology makes itself the prey of others that do not. At best it will fail to achieve the self-sufficiency at which it aims – at worst it will suffer the fate of the Tasmanians. There is no escape from a world of predatory states.

14

RUSSIA IN THE VANGUARD

Russians have always equated becoming modern with being like 'the West'. The result has always been that they have been thrown back on the remains of Russia's un-Western past.

Lenin's Bolsheviks were the most methodical of Russia's Westernisers. Their goal was to reorganise agriculture on the model of a nineteenth-century Western factory. The dash to industrialisation that followed destroyed Russian farming. In late Tsarist times, Russia was the world's largest grain exporter. Under the Soviet system the country's food supply came from small allotments run by former peasants. The end result of communist modernisation was to return Russians to subsistence farming.

It might be thought that this experiment would not be repeated. But when the Soviet regime collapsed, the Yeltsin government – heavily influenced by Western transnational agencies – again adopted a Western model. 'Shock therapy' was used to import an Anglo-Saxon free market into Russia. Given the state of Russian industry – a vast military-industrial

rustbelt – this was impossible. In the event, the Russian economy plunged into a profound depression. For most people in
the countryside and many in the cities, only smallholdings
staved off starvation.

Every attempt to modernise Russia on a Western model
has failed. That does not mean Russia is not modern. Quite
to the contrary, it has pioneered what may prove to be the
most advanced form of capitalism. A hypermodern economy
has arisen from the ashes of the Soviet state – a mafia-based
anarcho-capitalism that is expanding throughout the West.
The globalisation of Russian organised crime occurs at a
time when illegal industries – drugs, pornography, prostitu-
tion, cyber-fraud and the like – are the true growth sectors in
the most advanced economies. Russian anarcho-capitalism
shows many signs of surpassing Western capitalism in this
new phase of development.

Formerly the site of many failed projects of Western-
isation, Russia is today in the vanguard of modernisation
in the West.

15

'WESTERN VALUES'

When communism collapsed, most Russians longed for nothing more than to join 'the West'. Their reward was to be
treated worse than the Axis powers at the end of the Second
World War.

Ever since it rejected Maoism – an attempt to remake the country on a Soviet, which is to say a Western, model – China has shown an unwavering contempt for Western advice. As a result, China is fêted by the West as a haven of economic stability and good government.

Japan was the first non-Western country to modernise, but it remains radically un-Western to this day. A far smaller proportion of the population is in jail in Japan than in any Western country – around a twentieth of that in the United States. Evidently the Japanese have yet to embrace Western values.

16

FUTURE WAR

If you want to understand twenty-first-century wars, forget the ideological conflicts of the twentieth century. Read Malthus instead. Future wars will be fought over dwindling natural resources.

The genocidal war between Hutus and Tutsis in Rwanda had several causes, not least the deformation of the country's tribal cultures by its Belgian colonial rulers. But it was partly a struggle for water. E. O. Wilson writes:

> On the surface it would seem, and was so reported by the media, that the Rwandan catastrophe was ethnic rivalry run amok. That is true only in part. There was a

deeper cause, rooted in environment and demography. Between 1950 and 1994, the population of Rwanda, favoured by better health care and temporarily improved food supply, more than tripled, from 2.5 million to 8.5 million. In 1992, the country had the highest growth rate in the world, an average of 8 children for every woman. . . . though total food production improved dramatically during this period, it was soon overbalanced by population growth. . . . Per capita grain production fell by half from 1960 to the early nineties. Water was so overdrawn that hydrologists declared Rwanda one of the world's twenty-seven water-stressed countries. The teenage soldiers of the Hutu and Tutsi set out to solve the population problem in the most direct way.

Do not make the mistake of thinking that wars of scarcity are fought only among the poor. The wealth of the richest countries depends on retaining their grip on natural resources. In Central Asia the Great Game has been resumed, with the great powers vying for control of oil as they did in the nineteenth century. In the Persian Gulf, poor and rapidly growing populations need high and rising oil prices to survive. At the same time, rich countries need stable or falling oil prices if they are to continue to prosper. The result is a classical Malthusian conflict.

The Cold War was a family quarrel among Western ideologies. Whatever else they may be, future wars will be wars of scarcity. Waged against the world's modern states by the stateless armies of the militant poor, they are certain to be hugely destructive. We may well look back on the twentieth century as a time of peace.

17

WAR AS PLAY

Recalling an English railway station during the First World War, Bertrand Russell wrote that it 'was crowded with soldiers, almost all of them drunk, half of them accompanied by drunken prostitutes, the other half by wives or sweethearts, all despairing, all reckless, all mad'. It was such experiences that compelled Russell to revise his view of human nature: 'I had supposed that most people liked money better than anything else, but I discovered that they liked destruction even better.'

Russell's epiphany came from glimpsing a truth not admitted in his rationalistic philosophy. He believed fulfilment was in love, the pursuit of truth and working for a better world. What he saw in the departing soldiers was that, for average humanity, happiness is found in none of these things, but in the desperate, world-forgetting play of war.

War and play have long been linked. In Homeric Greek, *agon* signifies the rivalry of sport and the mortal combat of war. Both are games, and – save for the glory that comes with triumph or death – neither has an end beyond itself. In Homeric and pre-Socratic times, Spariosu writes, *agon* was a cosmic principle which 'governs the transactions among heroes, among gods, between men and gods, and between mortals and Moira [fate]'. The *Iliad* is the story of a war game, played out by mortals for the amusement of the gods. In Heraclitus's *Fragments*, the world itself is 'a child at play, moving pieces in a game. Kingship belongs to the child.'

Wars are not fought to stave off boredom. They come from ethnic and religious enmities, competition for trade and territory, the life-and-death struggle for scarce resources. But once it is under way, war is often embraced as a release. Like tyranny, it promises to cut the cord of circumstance that tethers average humanity to its chores. As with tyranny, the promise is fraudulent; but the jobbing world is broken up, its spent hopes and empty duties left behind for a time. If war is celebrated, it is because for much of humankind it stands for a dream of freedom.

In the *Iliad*, death in war is celebrated in song. Unlike Homer, we cannot admit the link between war and play. Yet war remains a game. Among bored consumers in rich post-military societies, it has become another entertainment. As for real war, that is like smoking, a habit of the poor.

18

YET ANOTHER UTOPIA

We can dream of a world in which a greatly reduced human population lives in a partially restored paradise; in which farming has been abandoned, and green deserts given back to the earth; where the remaining humans are settled in cities, emulating the noble idleness of hunter-gatherers, their needs met by new technologies that leave little mark on the Earth; where life is given over to curiosity, pleasure and play.

There is nothing technically impossible about such a world. New technologies cannot undo the laws of thermodynamics; but they can be friendlier to the Earth than the old technologies. Microchips allow technology to be partially dematerialised, making it less energy-intensive. Solar power allows energy consumption to be partly decarbonised, reducing its environmental impact. James Lovelock has suggested using nuclear power to counter global warming. E. O. Wilson has proposed that genetically modified foods have a role in a far-reaching programme of conservation and population control.

A high-tech Green utopia, in which a few humans live happily in balance with the rest of life, is scientifically feasible; but it is humanly unimaginable. If anything like it ever comes about, it will not be through the will of *homo rapiens*.

So long as population grows, progress will consist in labouring to keep up with it. There is only one way that humanity can limit its labours, and that is by limiting its numbers. But limiting human numbers clashes with powerful human needs. The Kurds and the Palestinians see large numbers of children as a survival strategy. Where communities are locked in intractable conflict, a high birth rate is a weapon. In any future we can realistically foresee, there will be many such conflicts. Zero population growth could be enforced only by a global authority with draconian powers and unwavering determination. There never has been such a power, and there never will be.

And yet . . . What if a shift in our place in the world were to come about without anyone planning it? What if our designs for the future were moves in a game in which we are only passing players?

19

POSTHUMAN EVOLUTION

Nearly one hundred and fifty years ago, Samuel Butler wrote: 'It appears to us that we are ourselves creating our own successors . . . giving them greater power and supplying by all sorts of ingenious contrivance that self-regulating, self-acting power which will be to them what intellect has been to the human race.'

Humans are no more masters of machines than they are of fire or the wheel. The forms of artificial life and intelligence they are constructing today will elude human control just as naturally occurring forms of life have done. They may even replace their creators.

Natural life forms have no built-in evolutionary advantage over organisms that began their life as artefacts. Adrian Woolfson writes: 'it is by no means certain that living things constructed from natural biological materials would be able to out-compete their synthetic and ahistorically designed, machine-based rivals'. Digital evolution – natural selection among virtual organisms in cyberspace – may already be at work. Soon telephone exchanges may be run by living software. But the new virtual environment is no more controllable than the natural world. According to Mark Ward, 'once a system is handed over to living, breeding software there is no turning back'.

The fear that humans could be supplanted by machines is voiced by Bill Joy, one of the architects of microprocessors: '. . . now, with the prospect of human-level computers in about 30 years, a new idea suggests itself: that I may be working to create tools which will enable the construction of the technology that may replace our species. How do I feel about this? Very uncomfortable.' While condemning his actions, Joy echoes Theodore Kaczynski, the Unabomber, who wrote of his despair at humans being 'reduced to the status of domestic animals'.

The replacement of humanity by its own artefacts is a curious prospect. But could the more highly evolved offspring of human artefacts be more destructive of other forms of life than humans themselves? Humans could soon find themselves in an impoverished environment different from any in which they have ever lived. Almost inevitably, they will seek to remodel themselves, the better to survive in the wasteland they have made. Benign bio-engineers may seek to remove the genes that carry biophilia – the primordial feeling for other living things that links humans with their evolutionary home.

Only a breed of ex-humans can thrive in the world that unchecked human expansion is creating. If humans were side-lined by machines and driven like today's hunter-gatherers to the edges of the world, would that be a worse fate?

20

THE SOUL IN THE MACHINE

Those who fear conscious machines do so because they think that consciousness is the most valuable feature of humans – and because they fear anything they cannot subject to their will. They fear the evolution of conscious machines for the same reason they seek to become masters of the Earth.

As machines slip from human control they will do more than become conscious. They will become spiritual beings, whose inner life is no more limited by conscious thought than ours. Not only will they think and have emotions, they will develop the errors and illusions that go with self-awareness.

Thinking machines will surely have languages of their own. They will not be artificial languages, which convey only the conscious thoughts of their makers, but natural languages, no less rich and obscure than our own. Natural languages contain more meaning than their users can ever express. The vernacular languages of machines will soon be more eloquent than the artificial languages of humans.

Esperanto was meant to be a transparent medium for our thoughts; but if it ever comes to be as widely spoken as

English it will be just as opaque. In the same way, the artificial intelligences we are now devising will evolve to talk to one another – and to us – in ways no one fully understands. Like us, the talking machines of the future will find themselves saying more than they can ever tell.

Everyone asks whether machines will someday be able to think as humans do. Few ask whether machines will ever think like cats or gorillas, dolphins or bats. Scientists searching for extra-terrestrial life ponder anxiously whether mankind is alone in the universe. They would be better occupied trying to communicate with the dwindling numbers of their animal kin.

Descartes described animals as machines. The great cogitator would have been nearer the truth if he had described himself as a machine. Consciousness may be the human attribute that machines can most easily reproduce. It may be in their capacity for consciousness that humans and the machines they are now devising are most alike.

The digital world was invented as an extension of human consciousness, but it soon transcended it. In future, the digital world will outreach even the minds of machines. The virtual universe created by the World Wide Web cannot be grasped by any mind. According to George Dyson, 'No digital universe can ever be completely mapped.' New technologies are creating a new wilderness, a realm that humans can wander in without ever understanding. The emergence of a virtual wilderness does not compensate for the loss of the earthly one that humans are destroying; but it is like it in being unknowable by them. The new wilderness is a pathway leading beyond the borders of the human world. As Margulis and Sagan have written: 'the Gaian meaning of technology reveals itself: as a human-mediated but not a human phenomenon, whose applications stand to expand the influence of all life on Earth, not just humanity'.

As machines evolve, they will come – to use a way of speaking that long predates Christianity – to have souls. In the words of Santayana: 'Spirit is itself not human; it may spring up in any life; it may detach itself from any provincialism; as it exists in all nations and religions, so it may exist in all animals, and who knows in many undreamt-of beings, and in the midst of what worlds?'

Throughout history and prehistory, animists have believed that matter is full of spirit. Why not welcome the living proof of this ancient faith?

6
AS IT IS

... should the truth about the world exist, it's bound to be nonhuman.

JOSEPH BRODSKY

1

THE CONSOLATIONS OF ACTION

In his novel *Nostromo*, Joseph Conrad wrote: 'Action is consolatory. It is the enemy of thought and the friend of flattering illusions.'

For those for whom life means action, the world is a stage on which to enact their dreams. Over the past few hundred years, at least in Europe, religion has waned, but we have not become less obsessed with imprinting a human meaning on things. A thin secular idealism has become the dominant attitude to life. The world has come to be seen as something to be remade in our own image. The idea that the aim of life is not action but contemplation has almost disappeared.

Those who struggle to change the world see themselves as noble, even tragic figures. Yet most of those who work for world betterment are not rebels against the scheme of things. They seek consolation for a truth they are too weak to bear. At bottom, their faith that the world can be transformed by human will is a denial of their own mortality.

Wyndham Lewis described the idea of progress as 'time-worship' – the belief that things are valuable not for what they are but for what they may someday become. In fact it is the opposite. Progress promises release from time – the hope that, in the spiralling ascent of the species, we can somehow preserve ourselves from oblivion.

Action preserves a sense of self-identity that reflection dispels. When we are at work in the world we have a seeming solidity. Action gives us consolation for our inexistence. It is not the idle dreamer who escapes from reality. It is practical men and women, who turn to a life of action as a refuge from insignificance.

Today the good life means making full use of science and technology – without succumbing to the illusion that they can make us free, reasonable, or even sane. It means seeking peace – without hoping for a world without war. It means cherishing freedom – in the knowledge that it is an interval between anarchy and tyranny.

The good life is not found in dreams of progress, but in coping with tragic contingencies. We have been reared on religions and philosophies that deny the experience of tragedy. Can we imagine a life that is not founded on the consolations of action? Or are we too lax and coarse even to dream of living without them?

2

SISYPHUS'S PROGRESS

Nothing is more alien to the present age than idleness. If we think of resting from our labours, it is only in order to return to them.

In thinking so highly of work we are aberrant. Few other cultures have ever done so. For nearly all of history and all prehistory, work was an indignity.

Among Christians, only Protestants have ever believed that work smacks of salvation; the work and prayer of medieval Christendom were interspersed with festivals. The ancient Greeks sought salvation in philosophy, the Indians in meditation, the Chinese in poetry and the love of nature. The pygmies of the African rainforests – now nearly extinct – work only to meet the needs of the day, and spend most of their lives idling.

Progress condemns idleness. The work needed to deliver humanity is vast. Indeed it is limitless, since as one plateau of achievement is reached another looms up. Of course this is only a mirage; but the worst of progress is not that it is an illusion. It is that it is endless.

In Greek myth, Sisyphus struggles to roll a stone to the top of a hill so it will then roll down the other side. Robert Graves tells his story thus:

He has never yet succeeded in doing so. As soon as he has almost reached the summit, he is forced back by the weight of the shameless stone, which bounces to the

very bottom once more; where he wearily retrieves it
and must begin all over again, though sweat bathes his
limbs, and a cloud of dust rises above his head.

For the ancients, unending labour was the mark of a slave.
The labours of Sisyphus are a punishment. In working for
progress we submit to a labour no less servile.

3

PLAYING WITH FATE

Gamblers wager for the sake of playing. Among those who
fish for pleasure, the best fisherman is not the one who
catches the most fish but the one who enjoys fishing the most.
The point of playing is that play has no point.

How can there be play in a time where nothing has meaning unless it leads to something else? In our eyes, *Homo ludens*
lives a life without purpose. Since play is beyond us, we have
given ourselves over to a life of purposeless work instead. To
labour as Sisyphus does is our fate.

But can we make our labours more playful? At present
we think of science and technology as means of mastering
the world. But the self that struggles to master the world
is only a shimmer on the surface of things. The new technologies that are springing up around us seem to be
inventions that serve our ends, when they and we are moves
in a game that has no end.

Technology obeys no one's will. Can we play along with it without labouring to master it?

4

TURNING BACK

Searching for a meaning in life may be useful therapy, but it has nothing to do with the life of the spirit. Spiritual life is not a search for meaning but a release from it.

Plato believed the end of life was contemplation. Action had value only in making contemplation possible; but contemplation meant communing with a human idea. Like many mystical thinkers, Plato thought of the world disclosed by the senses as a realm of shadows. Values were the ultimate realities. In contemplation Plato sought union with the highest value – the Good.

For Plato, as for the Christians who followed him, reality and the Good were one. But the Good is a makeshift of hope and desire, not the truth of things. Values are only human needs, or the needs of other animals, turned into abstractions. They have no reality in themselves, as George Santayana points out:

All animals have within them a principle by which to distinguish good from evil, since their existence and welfare are furthered by some circumstances and acts and are hindered by others. Self-knowledge, with a little experience of the world, will then easily set up the Socratic standard of values natural and inevitable to any man or to any society. These values each society will disentangle in proportion to its intelligence and will defend in proportion to its vitality. But who would dream that *spiritual life* was at all concerned in asserting these human and local values, or in supposing that they were especially divine, or bound to dominate the universe for ever?

Through fasting, concentration and prayer, mystics shut out the shifting world of the senses in order to reach a timeless reality. Quite often they find what they seek – but it is only a shadow play, an arabesque of their own anxieties, projected onto an inner screen. They end as they began, stuck fast in the personal time of memory and regret.

In modern times, the immortal longings of the mystics are expressed in a cult of incessant activity. Infinite progress . . . infinite tedium. What could be more dreary than the perfection of mankind? The idea of progress is only the longing for immortality given a techno-futurist twist. Sanity is not found here, nor in the moth-eaten eternities of the mystics.

Other animals do not pine for a deathless life. They are already in it. Even a caged tiger passes its life half out of time. Humans cannot enter that never-ending moment. They can find a respite from time when – like Odysseus, who refused Calypso's offer of everlasting life on an enchanted island so he could return to his beloved home – they no longer dream of immortality.

Contemplation is not the willed stillness of the mystics but a willing surrender to never-returning moments. When we turn away from our all-too-human yearnings we turn back to mortal things. Not moral hopes or mystical dreams but groundless facts are the true objects of contemplation.

5

SIMPLY TO SEE

Other animals do not need a purpose in life. A contradiction to itself, the human animal cannot do without one. Can we not think of the aim of life as being simply to see?

FURTHER READING

1 THE HUMAN

Jacques Monod, *Chance and Necessity*, London, Collins, 1971.

E. O. Wilson, *Consilience: The Unity of Knowledge*, London, Abacus, 1998, which includes a discussion of the Eremozoic Era, as well as a forceful critique of the belief that humans are exempt from the processes that govern the lives of all other animals.

For an overview of the scientific controversies surrounding the last mass extinction, see M. Benton, 'Scientific Methodologies in Collision: A History of the Study of the Extinction of the Dinosaurs', *Evolutionary Biology*, Vol. 24, 1990.

E. O. Wilson, *In Search of Nature*, London, Penguin Books, 1998.

Jared Diamond, *The Rise and Fall of the Third Chimpanzee: How Our Animal Heritage Affects the Way We Live*, London, Vintage, 1992.

On the Russian demographic collapse, see my book *False Dawn: The Delusions of Global Capitalism*, London and New York, Granta Books and New Press, 1998.

On population growth projections, see the report of Austria's International Institute for Applied Systems Analysis, cited in 'Ageing Planet', *Guardian*, 2 August 2001.

Reg Morrison, *The Spirit in the Gene: Humanity's Proud Illusion and the Laws of Nature*, Ithaca and London, Cornell University Press, 1999. Morrison's own belief is that population will fail to reach even the lowest UN projection of 7.7 billion by 2050.

James Lovelock, *Gaia: The Practical Science of Planetary Medicine*, London, Gaia Books, 1991. This includes a canonical exposition of the science of geophysiology.

Lynn Margulis, *The Symbiotic Planet: A New Look at Evolution*, London, Weidenfeld and Nicolson, 1998.

On the effects of climate change on countries such as Bangladesh, see the report on the United Nations Intergovernmental Panel on Environmental Change in the *Independent*, 14 November 2000.

For epidemiological interpretations of history, see Hans Zinsser, *Rats, Lice and History*, New York, Bantam, 1935; William McNeill, *Plagues and Peoples*, Harmondsworth, Penguin, 1979; Michael B. A. Oldstone, *Viruses, Plagues and History*, Oxford, Oxford University Press, 1998.

Thomas Malthus, *An Essay on the Principle of Population*, ed. Anthony Flew, Harmondsworth, Penguin, 1970.

Report from Iron Mountain on the Possibility and Desirability of Peace, with introductory material by Leonard C. Lewin, Harmondsworth, Penguin, 1968. The report was a spoof, with Lewin its author.

Bill Joy, 'Why the Future Doesn't Need Us', *Wired*, April 2000.

For an account of the twentieth century's largest covert biological weapons programme by one of the men who ran it in the former Soviet Union, see Ken Alibek (with Stephen Handleman), *Biohazard*, London, Arrow Books, 2000.

Ivan D. Illich, *Energy and Equity*, London, Calder and Boyars, 1974.

For a poetic vision of the place of the automobile in contemporary life, see Heathcote Williams, *Autogeddon*, London, Jonathan Cape, 1991.

Brian J. Ford, *Sensitive Souls: Senses and Communication in Plants, Animals and Microbes*, London, Warner Books, 1999.

Lynn Margulis and Dorion Sagan, 'Marvellous Microbes', *Resurgence*, No. 206, May/June 2001.

Bertrand Russell, *The Scientific Outlook*, London, George Allen and Unwin Ltd., 1931.

Paul Feyerabend, *Against Method*, London, New Left Books, 1975. For a powerful and witty demolition of Popper's philosophy of science, see Feyerabend's 'Trivializing Knowledge: Comments on Popper's Excursions into Philosophy', in *Farewell to Reason*, London and New York, Verso, 1987. For the social and historical context of scientific discovery, see Bruno Latour, *We Have Never Been Modern*, trans. Catherine Porter, London and New York, Prentice-Hall, 1993, Chapter 1.

Paul Feyerabend, *Conquest of Abundance: A Tale of Abstraction versus the Richness of Being*, Chicago and London, University of Chicago Press, 1999, especially pp. 131–60.

Julian Barbour, *The End of Time*, London, Phoenix, 1999.

On Socrates, see E. R. Dodds, *The Greeks and the Irrational*, Berkeley and London, University of California Press, 1951, p. 195.

On shamanism, see Mircea Eliade, *Shamanism: Archaic Techniques of Ecstasy*, London and New York, Routledge and Kegan Paul, 1972. For the influence of shamanic practices on Socrates and Plato, see Dodds, Chapter 5.

See Richard Dawkins, *The Selfish Gene*, Oxford and New York, Oxford University Press, 1990, for the idea of memes. Robert Trivers's Foreword discusses the idea that evolution favours useful error.

Bernd Heinrich, *Mind of the Raven: Investigations and Adventures with Wolf-Birds*, New York, Harper Perennial/Cliff Street Books, 2000.

Robert Wright, *The Moral Animal: Evolutionary Psychology and Everyday Life*, New York, Pantheon Books, 1994, especially Chapter 13.

Robinson Jeffers, 'Theory of Truth', in *The Collected Poetry of Robinson Jeffers*, Vol. 2, *1928–1938*, ed. Tim Hunt, Stanford, Cal., Stanford University Press, 1989.

Blaise Pascal, *Pensées*, London, Penguin, 1966.

The Daisyworld model is discussed in James Lovelock, *The Ages of Gaia: A Biography of Our Living Earth*, Oxford, Oxford University Press, 1989, Chapters 2–3. Lovelock has considered some conventional objections to the Daisyworld model in his book, *Gaia: The Practical Science of*

Planetary Medicine, London, Gaia Books, 1991. See also his *Homage to Gaia: The Life of an Independent Scientist*, Oxford, Oxford University Press, 2000.

Joel de Rosnay, *The Symbiotic Man*, London and New York, McGraw Hill, 2000.

For an illuminating philosophical examination of Gaia theory, see Mary Midgley, *Gaia – The Next Big Idea*, London, Demos, 2001.

Lao Tzu, *Tao Te Ching*, trans. D. C. Lau, London, Penguin Books, 1964.

2   THE DECEPTION

F. Nietzsche, *Joyful Wisdom*, New York, Frederick Ungar Publishing Co., 1960.

A. Schopenhauer, *On the Basis of Morality*, trans. E.J.F. Payne, Indianapolis and New York, Library of Liberal Arts, Bobbs-Merrill Co. Inc., 1965.

Rudiger Safranski, *Schopenhauer and the Wild Years of Philosophy*, London, Weidenfeld and Nicolson, 1989.

A. Schopenhauer, 'On Women', in *Parerga and Paralipomena*, Vol. 2, trans. E.J.F. Payne, Oxford, Clarendon Press, 1980.

For an interesting exploration of Greek Scepticism and the practical possibilities and difficulties of living as a sceptic today, see Arne Naess, *Scepticism*, London and New York, Routledge and Kegan Paul, 1968.

The best introduction to Schopenhauer's philosophy remains that of Patrick Gardiner, *Schopenhauer*, Harmondsworth, Penguin Books, 1963.

Schopenhauer recognises the closeness of his thinking to Vedantic philosophy in a number of places. For examples, see *Parerga and Paralipomena*, Vol. 2.

A. Schopenhauer, *The World as Will and Representation*, trans. E.J.F. Payne, Vol. 2, New York, Dover Publications, 1966.

Walter F. Otto, *Dionysus: Myth and Cult*, trans. Robert B. Palmer, Bloomington and Indianapolis, Indiana University Press, 1965.

On Nietzsche's final breakdown, see Lesley Chamberlain's brilliant account, *Nietzsche in Turin: The End of the Future*, London, Quartet, 1996. For a detailed account of Nietzsche's last days, see E. F. Podach, *The Madness of Nietzsche*, trans. F. A. Voigt, London and New York, Putnam, 1931. For an excellent recent biography of Nietzsche, see Rudiger Safranski, *Nietzsche: A Philosophical Biography*, New York and London, W. W. Norton and Company and Granta Books, 2001.

For Heidegger's account of the 'world-poverty' of other animals, see David Farrell Krell, *Daimon Life: Heidegger and Life-Philosophy*, Bloomington and Indianapolis, Indiana University Press, 1992. For an incisive critique of Heidegger's account, see Alasdair MacIntyre, *Dependent Rational Animals: Why Human Beings Need the Virtues*, London, Duckworth, 1999.

Martin Heidegger, *Basic Writings*, ed. David Farrell Krell, London and Henley, Routledge and Kegan Paul, 1978.

For a definitive argument that Heidegger's account of Being is secular Christianity, see Herman Philipse, *Heidegger's Philosophy of Being: A Critical Interpretation*, Princeton, Princeton University Press, 1998. For Heidegger's debts to Meister Eckardt and Angelus Silesius, see John D. Caputo, *The Mystical Element in Heidegger's Thought*, New York, Fordham University Press, 1986. For a comparison of Heidegger's way of thinking with Gnosticism, see Hans Jonas, *The Gnostic Religion: The Message of the Alien God and the Beginnings of Christianity*, 2nd edn, Boston, Beacon Press, 1958.

For Heidegger's conception of *Gelassenheit* (releasement), see his *Discourse on Thinking*, New York, Harper, 1966.

The quote from Heidegger's November 1933 speech comes from Rudiger Safranski's superb *Martin Heidegger: Between Good and Evil*, Cambridge, Mass., and London, Harvard University Press, 1998.

For Karl Lowith's first-hand account of Heidegger's Nazism, see his 'My Last Meeting with Heidegger in Rome, 1936', in R. Wolin, *The Heidegger Controversy: A Critical Reader*, Cambridge, Mass., and London, MIT Press, 1993. See also Karl Lowith, ed. R. Wolin, *Martin Heidegger and European Nihilism*, trans. Gary Steiner, New York, Columbia University Press, 1995.

See Reinhard May, *Heidegger's Hidden Sources: East Asian Influences on His Work*, trans. Graham Parkes, London and New York,

Routledge, 1996. For discussions of Heidegger's relations with Asian thought, see M. Sprung, ed., *The Question of Being*, University Park and London, Pennsylvania State University Press, 1978, and Graham Parkes, ed., *Heidegger and Asian Thought*, Honolulu, University of Hawaii Press, 1987.

Wittgenstein's comment on lions is to be found in his *Philosophical Investigations*, Oxford, Basil Blackwell, 1989. John Aspinall's reply was given in conversation with the author. Aspinall was a pioneer in showing that barriers between humans and other animals could be overcome and relations of friendship and trust formed across species. See John Aspinall, *The Best of Friends*, London, Macmillan, 1976.

For a interesting and off-beat introduction to Wittgenstein, see K. T. Fann, *Wittgenstein's Conception of Philosophy*, Berkeley and Los Angeles, University of California Press, 1969. Fann's collection of essays by various writers, *Ludwig Wittgenstein: The Man and His Philosophy*, New Jersey and Sussex, Humanities Press and Harvester Press, 1978, is also worth reading. For a discussion of the historical and cultural context of Wittgenstein's thought, see B. MacGuinness, *Wittgenstein and His Times*, Oxford, Basil Blackwell, 1982. For a magnificent account of Wittgenstein's life and character, see Ray Monk, *Wittgenstein: The Duty of Genius*, London, Penguin, 1991.

Amongst postmodernist writers, Richard Rorty and Michel Foucault are most worth reading. See Richard Rorty, *Contingency, Irony and Solidarity*, Cambridge, Cambridge University Press, 1989, and Michel Foucault, *Madness and Civilisation*, London, Tavistock Methuen, 1967.

For the classic statement of the view that human knowledge is a sublimation of animal faith, see George Santayana's neglected masterpiece *Scepticism and Animal Faith*, New York, Dover Publications, 1955.

For a discussion of Mauthner and Wittgenstein, see Gershon Weiler, *Mauthner's Critique of Language*, Cambridge, Cambridge University Press, 1970.

A. C. Graham, *Disputers of the Tao: Philosophical Argument in Ancient China*, La Salle, Ill., Open Court, 1989. Graham notes an ancient Chinese idea of 'model' which resembles somewhat Western ideas of universals and forms, but concludes that it is 'in several respects profoundly different'.

In my view of Chinese thought as nominalist, I leave aside, though not because they are without interest, the ancient Chinese Legalists who tried to fix the meanings of words. For a brief account of the Legalist view of language, see Burton Watson, *Han Fei Tzu: Basic Writings*, New York, Columbia University Press, 1964, Introduction. For a more comprehensive discussion, see Chad Hansen, *A Daoist Theory of Chinese Thought: A Philosophical Interpretation*, New York and Oxford, Oxford University Press, 1992, Chapter 7.

Brian J. Ford, *Sensitive Souls: Senses and Communication in Plants, Animals and Microbes*, London, Warner Books, 1999.

Lynn Margulis, *The Symbiotic Planet: A New Look at Evolution*, London, Weidenfeld and Nicolson, 1998.

See Fritjof Capra, *The Web of Life: A New Synthesis of Mind and*

Matter, London, Flamingo, 1997, for discussions of cognition in bacteria and immune systems.

Humberto Maturana and Francisco Varela, *Autopoesis and Cognition*, Dordrecht, D. Reidel, 1980.

On the mental capacities of apes, see Franz de Waal, *The Ape and the Sushi Master: Cultural Reflections of a Primatologist*, New York, Basic Books, 2000.

The classic study on self-awareness and archery is by Eugen Herrigel, *Zen in the Art of Archery*, London, Routledge and Kegan Paul, 1953.

Rebecca Stone Miller, *Art of the Andes from Chavin to Inca*, London, Thames and Hudson, 1995.

N. K. Sandars, *Prehistoric Art in Europe*, 2nd edn, New Haven, Conn., and London, Yale University Press and Penguin Books, 1992 and 1985.

Anton Ehrenzweig, *The Hidden Order of Art: A Study in the Psychology of Artistic Imagination*, London, Weidenfeld and Nicolson, 1967.

Tor Norretranders, *The User Illusion: Cutting Consciousness Down to Size*, London and New York, Penguin Books, 1999.

See L. Weiskrantz, *Blindsight: A Case Study and Implications*, Oxford, Clarendon Press, 1986. Weiskrantz's study is cited by Norretranders.

Joseph Conrad, *Lord Jim*, New York, W. W. Norton and Co., 1968.

For a compelling argument against freedom of will, see Galen

Strawson, *Freedom and Belief*, Oxford, Oxford University Press, 1986. For an equally compelling argument that abandoning the idea of free will would radically alter our whole way of thinking about ourselves, see 'From Hope and Fear Set Free', in Isaiah Berlin, *Liberty*, ed. Henry Hardy, Oxford, Oxford University Press, 2002. The view that freedom of will is an illusion we cannot shake off is brilliantly defended by Saul Smilansky, *Free Will and Illusion*, Oxford, Clarendon Press, 2000.

Benjamin Libet, Curtis A. Gleason, Elwood W. Wright and Dennis K. Pearl, 'Time of Conscious Intention to Act in Relation to Onset of Cerebral Activity (Readiness-Potential)', *Brain*, 106 (1983). See also Benjamin Libet, 'Unconscious Cerebral Initiative and the Role of Conscious Will in Voluntary Action', *Behavioural and Brain Sciences* 8 (1985). The philosophical significance of Libet's work is discussed in Daniel Dennet, *Consciousness Explained*, London, Penguin, 1993. See also John Searle, *The Mystery of Consciousness*, New York, New York Review Press, 1997. For scientific research on consciousness that further undermines the Cartesian view, see Antonio Damasio, *The Feeling of What Happens: Body and Emotion in the Making of Consciousness*, New York, Harcourt Brace, 1999, and Damasio's *Descartes's Error: Emotion, Reason and the Human Brain*, New York, Grosset/Putnam, 1994.

I am grateful to Vincent Deary for information on the bandwidth of consciousness.

Arthur Schopenhauer, *The World as Will and Representation*, trans. E.J.F. Payne, Vol. 2, New York, Dover Publications, 1966.

On coping, see Mark Wrathall and Jeff Malpas, eds., *Heidegger, Coping and Cognitive Science: Essays in Honour of Hubert L. Dreyfus*, 2 vols., Cambridge, Mass., and London, MIT Press, 2000, particularly Vol. 1, Chapters 1–6. See also Hubert L. Dreyfus's magnificent *Being-in-the-World: A Commentary on Heidegger's* Being and Time, *Division 1*, Cambridge, Mass., and London, MIT Press, 1991, which includes an account of knowing-how that is akin to that which I sketch in this book.

Francisco J. Varela, *Ethical Know-How: Action, Wisdom and Cognition*, Stanford, Stanford University Press, 1999. See also Humberto Maturana and Francisco J. Varela, *The Tree of Knowledge: The Biological Roots of Human Understanding*, Boston and London, Shambala, 1992.

R. A. Brooks, 'Achieving Artificial Intelligence Through Building Robots', *A.I. Memo 899*, Cambridge, Cambridge Artificial Intelligence Laboratory, May 1986.

See Eugene Marais, *The Soul of the White Ant*, London, Methuen, 1937. Marais's seminal work was plagiarised by the Flemish writer and Nobel Prize winner Maurice Maeterlinck in his book *The Life of the Ant*, published in Britain by Allen and Unwin, London, 1958. Marais committed suicide in 1936. For an account of this episode, see Robert Ardrey's Introduction to Marais's *The Soul of the Ape*, Harmondsworth, Penguin, 1969.

Goronwy Rees, *A Bundle of Sensations: Sketches in Autobiography*, London, Chatto and Windus, 1960. For a later account of his life, see Goronwy Rees, *A Chapter of Accidents*, London, Chatto and Windus, 1972.

David Hume, *A Treatise of Human Nature*, ed. L. A. Selby-Bigge and P. H. Nidditch, Oxford, Clarendon Press, 1978.

Jenny Rees, in *Mr Nobody: The Secret Life of Goronwy Rees*, London, Weidenfeld and Nicolson, 1994.

Gregory Bateson, 'A Theory of Play and Fantasy', in *Steps to an Ecology of Mind*, Chicago and London, University of Chicago Press, 2000.

Bernd Heinrich, *Mind of the Raven: Investigations and Adventures with Wolf-Birds*, New York, Harper Perennial/Cliff Street Books, 2000, especially Chapters 22 and 24.

For contemporary guides to Buddhist meditation, see A. Sole-Leris, *Tranquillity and Insight*, London, Rider, 1986, and Venerable Henepola Gunaratana, *Mindfulness in Plain English*, Boston, Wisdom Publications, 1993. For an interesting auto-biographical account of the practice of bare attention, see E. H. Shattock, *An Experiment in Mindfulness*, New York, Samuel Weiser, 1972.

For a study of lucid dreams and false awakenings, see Celia Green and Charles McCreery, *Lucid Dreaming: The Paradox of Consciousness during Sleep*, London and New York, Routledge, 1994.

For an illuminating study of Taoist mystical traditions, see Livia Kohn, *Early Chinese Mysticism: Philosophy and Soteriology in the Taoist Tradition*, Princeton, Princeton University Press, 1991.

The Book of Chuang-Tzu, trans. Martin Palmer and Elizabeth Breuilly, London, Penguin/Arkana, 1996. For commentaries on these sections of the *Chuang-Tzu*, see Robert E.

Allinson, *Chuang-Tzu for Spiritual Transformation: An Analysis of the Inner Chapters*, Albany, State University of New York Press, 1989, and Kuang-Ming Wu, *The Butterfly as Companion: Meditations on the First Three Chapters of the Chuang-Tzu*, Albany, State University of New York Press, 1990. See also Kuang-Ming Wu, *Chuang-Tzu: World Philosopher at Play*, New York, Crossroad Publishers and Scholars Press, 1982.

The Book of Lieh-Tzu, trans. A. C. Graham, London, Mandala, 1991.

Chuang-Tzu: The Inner Chapters, trans. A. C. Graham, London, Mandala/HarperCollins, 1991.

Pierre Hadot, *Philosophy as a Way of Life: Spiritual Exercises from Socrates to Foucault*, trans. M. Chase, Oxford, Blackwell, 1995.

L. Shestov, *In Job's Balances: On the Sources of the Eternal Truths*, Athens, Ohio University Press, 1975.

3   THE VICES OF MORALITY

George Christoph Lichtenberg, *Aphorisms*, London, Penguin, 1990.

Bruce Chatwin, *Utz*, London, Picador, 1989. Chatwin's character Utz appears to have been a fictive version of the life of an actual person, Rudolph Just, a Czech collector whom Chatwin had met. Just's hoard of European faience and Chinese and Japanese porcelain survived him, hidden in a council flat in Bratislava, only to be auctioned off at Sotheby's in London in December 2001.

Roman Frister, *The Cap, or the Price of a Life*, trans. Hillel Halkin, London, Weidenfeld and Nicolson, 1999.

On the Tasmanian genocide, see Reg Morrison, *The Spirit in the Gene: Humanity's Proud Illusion and the Laws of Nature*, Ithaca and London, Cornell University Press, 1999; and Jared Diamond, *The Rise and Fall of the Third Chimpanzee: How Our Animal Heritage Affects the Way We Live*, London, Vintage, 1992.

E. O. Wilson, *On Human Nature*, London, Penguin, 1978.

Arthur Koestler, *Arrival and Departure*, London, Jonathan Cape, 1943, reprinted by Penguin Books, Harmondsworth, 1971.

On the occultist input into Nazism, see Nicholas Goodrick-Clarke, *The Occult Roots of Nazism: The Ariosophists of Austria and Germany, 1890–1935; The Racist and Nationalist Fantasies of Guido von List and Jorg Lanz von Liebenfels and Their Influence on Nazi Ideology*, Wellbrough, Aquarian Press, 1985; and Dorothy M. Figueira, *The Exotic: A Decadent Quest*, Albany, State University of New York Press, 1994.

For a contemporary account of Hitler's nihilism, see Hermann Rauschning, *The Revolution of Nihilism: Warning to the West*, New York, Longman, Green and Co., 1939. Rauschning was a Prussian conservative and mayor of Danzig who for a time belonged to Hitler's inner circle. When his hostility to Hitler became known, a price was put on his head and he fled to the United States.

For his defence of 'liquidation', see G. B. Shaw, 'Capital Punishment', *Atlantic Monthly*, June 1948.

Eugene Lyons, *Assignment in Utopia*, New York, Harcourt Brace and Co., 1937.

M. Heller and A. Nekrich, *Utopia in Power: The History of the Soviet Union from 1917 to the Present*, New York, Summit Books, 1986.

Gil Elliot, *Twentieth Century Book of the Dead*, Harmondsworth, Penguin, 1972.

The *Guardian*, 7 July 2000, reprints the story of the death of Mary Turner from *George* magazine, July 2000. An exhibition of photographs of lynchings was shown at the New York Historical Society, July–August 2000.

M. Gimbutas, *The Goddesses and Gods of Old Europe, 6500–3500 BC: Myths and Cult Images*, London, Thames and Hudson, 1996. Nietzsche argued for the Dionysiac origins of tragedy in *The Birth of Tragedy*, London, Penguin, 1993. A similar view is presented by Carl Kerenyi in *Dionysos: Archetypal Image of Indestructible Life*, Princeton, Princeton University Press, 1976.

E. R. Dodds, 'Euripides the Irrationalist', *Classical Review*, XLIII, 1929. See also Dodds's seminal book, *The Greeks and the Irrational*, Berkeley, University of California Press, 1951.

Gustaw Herling, *Volcano and Miracle*, New York, Penguin Books, 1996, to which I owe my reconstruction of Shalamov's last days. Herling himself published one of the most striking accounts of the Soviet camps, *A World Apart*, trans. Andrzej Ciozkosz (Joseph Marek), New York, Arbor House, 1951.

Varlam Shalamov, *Kolyma Tales*, trans. John Glad, London, Penguin Books, 1994.

Ryszard Kapuscinski, *Imperium*, London, Granta, 1993.

Robert Conquest, *Kolyma: The Arctic Death Camps*, London, Macmillan, 1978, Chapter 9, 'The Death Roll'.

Czeslaw Milosz, 'To Robinson Jeffers', in his *Visions from San Francisco Bay*, New York, Farrar, Straus and Giroux, 1982.

A more systematic critique of Rawls's theory can be found in my book *Two Faces of Liberalism*, Cambridge and New York, Polity Press and the New Press, 2000, as well as a discussion of conflicts among the virtues.

George Santayana, *Obiter Scripta*, ed. J. Buchler and B. Schwartz, London and New York, Charles Scribner's Sons, 1936. Perhaps there is an exception to the rule that no moral philosopher has written a great novel – George Santayana's *The Last Puritan: A Memoir in the Form of a Novel*, Cambridge, Mass., and London, MIT Press, 1994.

For Aristotle on ethics among the dolphins, see Alasdair MacIntyre's brilliant *Dependent Rational Animals: Why Human Beings Need the Virtues*, London, Duckworth, 1999.

F. Nietzsche, *Daybreak: Thoughts on the Prejudices of Morality*, eds. M. Clark and B. Leiter, trans. R. J. Hollingdale, Cambridge, Cambridge University Press, 1997.

Chuang-Tzu: The Inner Chapters, trans. A. C. Graham, London, HarperCollins/Mandala, 1990.

A. C. Graham, *Disputers of the Tao: Philosophical Argument in Ancient China*, La Salle, Ill., Open Court, 1989.

The Book of Chuang-Tzu, trans. Martin Palmer and Elizabeth Breuilly, London, Penguin/Arkana, 1996.

The Book of Lieh-Tzu, trans. A. C. Graham, London, Mandala, 1991.

4 THE UNSAVED

E. M. Cioran, *The Trouble with Being Born*, trans. Richard Howard, London, Quartet Books, 1993.

For an interpretation of Jesus's teaching as a species of Cynicism, see Burton L. Mack, *The Lost Gospel of Q: The Book of Christian Origins*, San Francisco, HarperSanFrancisco, 1993.

J. L. Borges, 'Christ on the Cross', in *Selected Poems*, ed. Alexander Coleman, New York, Viking Penguin, 1999.

D. H. Lawrence, *The Escaped Cock*, edited with a commentary by Gerald M. Lacy, Santa Barbara, Black Sparrow Press, 1976. The same story was published under the title 'The Man Who Died', and can be found in D. H. Lawrence, *Love among the Haystacks and Other Stories*, Harmondsworth, Penguin, 1972.

N. Kazantzakis, *Report to Greco*, London, Faber and Faber, 1973.

Robinson Jeffers, 'Rearmament' and 'Meditation on Saviors', in *Selected Poems*, Manchester, Carcanet, 1987.

F. Dostoevsky, *The Brothers Karamazov*, ed. R. E. Matlaw, New York, W. W. Norton and Co., 1976.

D. H. Lawrence, *Selected Literary Criticism*, ed. A. Beal, London, Heinemann, 1967.

The Iliad of Homer, trans. Richard Lattimore, Chicago and London, University of Chicago Press, 1961, Book 7, lines 58–66.

E. M. Cioran, *The New Gods*, trans. Richard Howard, New York, Quadrangle/New York Times Book Co., 1974.

Cyril Connolly, *The Unquiet Grave: A Word Cycle by Palinurus*, London, Penguin, 2000.

Fernando Pessoa, *The Book of Disquiet*, trans. Richard Zenith, Carcanet, Manchester, 1991.

A brief account of Krishnamurti's teaching may be found in J. Krishnamurti, *Freedom from the Known*, Brocklewood Park, Krishnamurti Foundation, 1969. For accounts of Krishnamurti's life, see Roland Vernon, *Star in the East: Krishnamurti – The Invention of a Messiah*, London, Constable, 2000; and Aryel Sanat, *The Inner Life of Krishnamurti: Private Passion and Perennial Wisdom*, Wheaton, Ill., Theosophical Publishing House, 1999.

For Grotosky's use of Gurdjieff's work, see Jerzy Grotosky, 'A Kind of Volcano', in J. Needleman and G. Baker, eds., *Gurdjieff: Essays and Reflections on the Man and His Teaching*, New York, Continuum, 1997. For an assessment of the impact of Gurdjieff on the work of Peter Brook, see Basarab Nicolescu, 'Peter Brook and Traditional Thought', *Contemporary Theatre Review*, Vol. 7, 1997.

G. I. Gurdjieff, *Views from the Real World*, London, Arkana, 1984. Gurdjieff's main published work is *Beelzebub's Tales to His Grandson*, London and New York, Penguin/Arkana,

1999. For an account of Gurdjieff's teaching, see Michel Waldberg, *Gurdjieff: An Approach to His Teachings*, trans. S. Cox, London, Routledge and Kegan Paul, 1981. For an account of Gurdjieff's life and circle, see James Webb, *The Harmonious Circle: The Lives and Work of G. I. Gurdjieff, P. D. Ouspensky, and Their Followers*, New York, G. P. Putnam's Sons, 1980. The ironies that come with attempting to follow Gurdjieff's injunction to become ever more conscious are evident in Henri Thomasson, *The Pursuit of the Present: Journal of Twenty Years in the Gurdjieff Work*, trans. Rina Hands, Amersham, Avebury Publishing Company, 1980.

Constantin Stanislavsky, *Creating a Role*, London, Methuen, 1988.

Rex Warner, *The Aerodrome*, Oxford and New York, Oxford University Press, 1982. The first edition of the book was published by Penguin in March 1941.

Dmitry Shlapentokh, 'Bolshevism as a Fedorovian Regime', *Cahiers du Monde Russe*, XXXVII(4), October–November 1996. See also Michael Heim, *The Metaphysics of Virtual Reality*, Oxford, Oxford University Press, 1993.

Murray Feisbach, *Ecocide in the USSR*, New York, Basic Books, 1992.

Boris Komarov, *The Destruction of Nature in the Soviet Union*, London, Pluto Press, 1979.

For cryogenic immortalism, see Robert C. W. Ettinger, *The Prospect of Immortality*, New York, Doubleday, 1964, and *Man into Superman*, New York, St Martin's Press, 1972; Alan Harrington, *The Immortalist: How Science Could Give Human-*

ity Eternal Life, London, Panther Books, 1978; Damien Broderick, *The Last Mortal Generation: How Science Will Alter Our Lives in the Twenty-first Century*, Sydney, New Holland Publishers, 1999.

Havelock Ellis, 'Mescal: A New Artificial Paradise', *Contemporary Review*, January 1898. Cited in Mike Jay's excellent study *Emperors of Dreams: Drugs in the Nineteenth Century*, Sawtrey, Daedalus, 2000.

On the Pergouset cave paintings, see Ciaran Regan, *Intoxicating Minds*, London, Weidenfeld, 2000.

Richard Rudgley, *Lost Civilisations of the Stone Age*, London, Arrow Books, 1999.

Eugene Marais, *The Soul of the Ape*, Harmondsworth, Penguin, 1969. For later research confirming Marais's findings, see Ronald K. Sigel, *Intoxication: Life in Pursuit of Artificial Paradise*, New York and London, Simon and Schuster, 1989.

Paul Devereaux, *Symbolic Landscapes*, London, Penguin/Arkana, 1997; Henry Hobhouse, *Seeds of Change: Six Plants that Transformed Mankind*, London, Papermac, 1992; Alexander and Ann Shulgin, *Pikhal: A Chemical Love Story*, Berkeley, Transform Press, 1995; Richard Davenport-Hines, *The Pursuit of Oblivion: A Global History of Narcotics, 1500–2000*, London, Weidenfeld, 2002.

For a profound study of Gnosticism, see Hans Jonas, *The Gnostic Religion*, Boston, Beacon Press, 1963.

Jung's Seminar on Nietzsche's Zarathustra, abridged and edited by J. L. Jarrett, Princeton, Princeton University Press, 1998.

For a study of Jung as a latter-day Gnostic, see Robert A. Segal, *The Gnostic Jung*, London, Routledge, 1992.

I owe the quotation from the founder of the Extropian Institute to Hubert Dreyfus, *On the Internet*, London and New York, Routledge, 2001. The statement can be found at the website of the Extropian Institute, www.ct.heise.de/tp/english/inhalt/co/2041/1.html.

Ray Kurzweil, *The Age of Spiritual Machines: When Computers Exceed Human Intelligence*, New York, Penguin, 2000.

The idea of cyberspace as a domain of virtual realities is the basis of William Gibson's *Neuromancer*, London, HarperCollins, 1995. The dangers of virtual reality games have been explored in David Cronenberg's surreal and humorous film *eXistenZ*. For a summary and commentary on Cronenberg's films, including *eXistenZ*, see John Costello, *The Pocket Essential David Cronenberg*, Harpenden, www.pocketessentials.com, 2000. *eXistenZ* deploys ideas presented by Philip K. Dick in his book *The Three Stigmata of Palmer Eldritch*, London, Grafton Books, 1978. For a profound meditation on Cronenberg's films, see Iain Sinclair's *Crash: David Cronenberg's Post-mortem on J. G. Ballard's 'Trajectory of Fate'*, London, British Film Institute Publishing, 1999.

Stanislaw Lem, *Summa Technologiae*, Krakow, Wydawnictwo Literackie, 1964.

Stanislaw Lem, *A Stanislaw Lem Reader*, ed. Peter Swinski, Evanston, Ill., Northwestern Press, 1997.

On shamanism, see Mircea Eliade's seminal study *Shaman-*

ism: Archaic Techniques of Ecstasy, London and New York, Routledge and Kegan Paul, 1972. For path-breaking studies of lucid dreaming, see Charles McCreery, *Psychical Phenomena and the Physical World*, London, Hamish Hamilton, 1973, Chapter 1; Celia Green and Charles McCreery, *Lucid Dreaming: The Paradox of Consciousness during Sleep*, London and New York, Routledge, 1994. For philosophical reflections on lucid dreaming and similar anomalous states, see Charles McCreery, *Science, Philosophy and ESP*, Oxford, Institute of Psychophysical Research, 1967; Celia Green, *The Human Evasion*, Oxford, Institute of Psychophysical Research, 1977.

On the use of drugs by shamans, see M. J. Harner, ed., *Hallucinogens and Shamanism*, Oxford, Oxford University Press, 1973. See also G. Riechel-Dolmatoff, *The Sham and the Jaguar: A Study of Narcotic Drugs among the Indians of Colombia*, Philadelphia, Temple University Press, 1975; R. E. Schultes and A. Hoffman, *Plants of the Gods: Origins of Hallucinogen Use*, London, Hutchinson, 1980.

E. O. Wilson, *Consilience*, London, Abacus, 1999.

Peter Vitousek, Anne H. Erlich and Pamela Matson, 'Human Appropriation of the Products of Photosynthesis', *BioScience*, Vol. 36, No. 6 (1986), pp. 368–73.

The poem is attributed to Alberto Caeiro, another of Pessoa's heteronyms. See *Poems of Fernando Pessoa*, trans. and ed. Edwin Honig and Susan M. Brown, San Francisco, City Lights Books, 1998.

For a delightful picture of a posthuman world, see Dougal Dixon, *After Man: A Zoology of the Future*, New York, St Martin's Griffin, 1998. See also Michael Bolter, *Extinction, Evolution and the End of Man*, London, Fourth Estate, 2002.

5 NON-PROGRESS

Karl Kraus, *Half Truths and One-and-a-half Truths*, ed. Harry Zohn, Montreal, Engendra Press, 1976.

Colin Tudge, *Neanderthals, Bandits and Farmers: How Agriculture Really Began*, London, Weidenfeld and Nicolson, 1998.

Marshall Sahlins, *Stone Age Economics*, Hawthorne, N.Y., Aldine de Gruyter, 1972. For another pivotal book on the life of hunter-gatherers, see Richard B. Lee and Irven De Vore, *Man the Hunter*, Chicago, Aldine, 1968.

Hugh Brody, *The Other Side of Eden: Hunter-Gatherers, Farmers and the Shaping of the World*, London, Faber and Faber, 2000.

M. N. Chen and G. J. Armelagos, eds., *Paleopathology at the Origins of Agriculture*, New York, Academic Press, 1984; Jared Diamond, *The Rise and Fall of the Third Chimpanzee: How Our Animal Heritage Affects the Way We Live*, London, Vintage, 1992; Jared Diamond, *Guns, Germs and Steel*, London, Vintage, 1998.

Clive Ponting, *A Green History of the World: The Environment and the Collapse of Great Civilizations*, London and New York, Penguin, 1993. Paul R. Erlich, *Human Natures: Genes, Cultures and the Human Prospect*, Washington, D.C., and Covelo, Cal., Island Press, Shearwater Books, 2000.

For an account of industrialisation as a side effect of population growth, see Richard G. Wilkinson, *Poverty and Progress: An Ecological Model of Economic Development*, London, Methuen, 1973.

Hans Moravec, *Robot: Mere Machine to Transcendent Mind*, Oxford and New York, Oxford University Press, 2000.

See my book *False Dawn: The Delusions of Global Capitalism*, London and New York, Granta and the New Press, 2002, for a discussion of the role of neoliberal economic policies in the rise of the underclass. This book also contains further discussion of the proletarianisation of the American middle class; neoliberal shock therapy in Russia; Japan's economic modernisation; and the impact of the terrorist attacks of September 2001.

Jeremy Rifkin, *The End of Work: The Decline of the Global Labour Force and the Dawn of the Post-market Era*, New York, G. P. Putnam's Sons, 1995.

For a discussion of the redundancy of careers, see Fernando Flores and John Gray, *Entrepreneurship and the Wired Life: Work in the Wake of Careers*, London, Demos, 2000.

J. H. Prynne, 'Sketch for a Financial Theory of the Self', in *Poems*, Newcastle, Bloodaxe Books, Fremantle Arts Centre Press, 1999.

J. G. Ballard, *Cocaine Nights*, London, Flamingo, 1997.

J. G. Ballard, *Super-Cannes*, Flamingo, 2000. In the book's foreword, Ballard writes that Eden-Olympia is inspired by the landscaped business park of Sophia-Antipolis, a few miles to the north of Antibes. But this may be a double bluff. Eden-Olympia may be modelled on a place actually called Super-Cannes. See Charles Jennings, 'Future Block', *Daily Telegraph*, 21 October 2000.

Raoul Vaneigem, *The Revolution of Everyday Life*, London, Practical Paradise Publications, 1975. The epigraph to this translation of Vaneigem's *Traité de savoir-vivre à l'Usage des jeunes générations* is a quote from the seventeenth-century Ranter Jo Salmon. See Norman Cohn's seminal history of medieval chiliastic movements, *The Pursuit of the Millennium: Revolutionary Millenarians and Mystical Anarchists of the Middle Ages*, first published in 1957, expanded and revised edition, London, Paladin, 1970. Vaneigem cites Cohn in *Revolution of Everyday Life*. He has given a more complete account of the Brethren of the Free Spirit in Raoul Vaneigem, *The Movement of the Free Spirit: General Considerations and Firsthand Testimony Concerning Some Brief Flowerings of Life in the Middle Ages, the Renaissance and, Incidentally, Our Own Time*, New York, Zone Books, 1998.

For a psychological interpretation of alchemy, see C. G. Jung, *Psychology and Alchemy*, 2nd edn, London, Routledge, 1968, and Jung's *magnum opus*, *Mysterium Coniunctionis*, Bollingen Series XX, Princeton, Princeton University Press, 1989.

I have discussed late Tsarism, and also the mythical content of classical Marxism, in my book *Post-liberalism: Studies in Political Thought*, London and New York, Routledge, 1993.

Guy Debord, *Comments on the Society of the Spectacle*, London and New York, Verso, 1990. See Guy Debord, *The Society of the*

Spectacle, New York, Zone Books, 1994. For Debord's cryptic essay in autobiography, see G. Debord, *Panegyric*, trans. James Brook, London and New York, Verso, 1991. For a useful intellectual biography, see Ansell Jappe and Donald Nicholson-Smith, *Guy Debord*, Berkeley, University of California Press, 1999.

Debord's advertisement for an agent appeared in the *Times Literary Supplement*, 22 February 1991. See Greil Marcus, 'You Could Catch It', in Greil Marcus, *The Dustbin of History*, Cambridge, Mass., and London, Harvard University Press and Picador, 1995.

On nutrition levels and on Çatal Hüyük, see Richard Rudgley, *Lost Civilisations of the Stone Age*, London, Arrow Books, 1999.

Iain Sinclair, *Lud Heat*, London, Granta, 1998.

Noel Perrin, *Giving Up the Gun: Japan's Reversion to the Sword, 1543–1879*, Boston, Nonpareil Books, 1979. For an account of the adoption of Western science in Japan see Carmen Blacker, *The Japanese Enlightenment*, Cambridge, Cambridge University Press, 1969.

I predicted the failure of neoliberal shock therapy in Russia in my monograph *The Post-communist Societies in Transition*, London, Social Market Foundation, February 1994, republished in my book *Enlightenment's Wake: Politics and Culture at the Close of the Modern Age*, London and New York, Routledge, 1995, Chapter 5. For a definitive study of the catastrophic effects of shock therapy in Russia, see Peter Reddaway and Dmitri Glinski, *The Tragedy of Russia's*

Reforms: Market Bolshevism against Democracy, Washington, D.C., United States Institute of Peace Press, 2001.

Thomas Malthus, *An Essay on the Principle of Population*, ed. Anthony Flew, Harmondsworth, Penguin, 1970.

On the colonial roots of the Rwandan genocide, see Clive Ponting, *The Pimlico History of the Twentieth Century*, London, Pimlico, 1999: 'Belgian policy was to emphasise the "racial" differences and unashamedly to favour the Tutsi. By the late 1950s they provided 43 out of the 45 major chiefs and 549 out of the 559 sub-chiefs. The Hutu were removed from their traditional areas of control, especially over land. The Tutsi, as the local elite, were given preference in education by the Catholic Church. Gradually the Africans came to accept the "racial" divisions imposed by the Belgians, partly because they reflected the local division of power.' See also Mahmood Mamdami, *When Victims Become Killers: Colonialism, Nativism and Genocide in Rwanda*, London, James Curry, 2001.

E. O. Wilson, *Consilience: The Unity of Knowledge*, London, Abacus, 1998.

The Autobiography of Bertrand Russell, Vol. 2, *1914–1944*, London, George Allen and Unwin, 1971.

For a discussion of the link between war and play, see J. Huizinga, *Homo Ludens: A Study of the Play-Element in Culture*, Boston, Beacon Press, 1986, Chapter 5.

Mihai I. Spariosu, *God of Many Names: Play, Poetry and Power in Hellenistic Thought from Homer to Aristotle*, Durham and London, Duke University Press, 1991. For a comprehensive survey of the concept of play, see Spariosu's *Dionysus Reborn: Play and the Aesthetic Dimension in Modern Philosophical and Scientific Discourse*, Ithaca and London, Cornell University Press, 1989.

Charles H. Kahn, *The Art and Thought of Heraclitus: An Edition of the Fragments with Translation and Commentary*, Cambridge, Cambridge University Press, 1979. A freer translation of the *Fragments* may be found in Guy Davenport, *Herakleitos and Diogenes*, San Francisco, Grey Fox Press, 1983.

Ivan Illich, *Tools for Conviviality*, London, Calder and Boyars, 1973.

For Lovelock's views on nuclear power, see James Lovelock, *The Ages of Gaia: A Biography of Our Living Earth*, Oxford, Oxford University Press, 1989.

For E. O. Wilson's views on GMOs, see 'Darwin's Natural Heir', *Guardian*, 17 February 2001.

Samuel Butler, *A First Year in Canterbury Settlement*, London, Longman and Green, 1863, quoted in George Dyson's brilliant book *Darwin among the Machines*, London, Penguin Books, 1997.

Adrian Woolfson, *Life without Genes: The History and Future of Genomes*, London, Flamingo, 2000, p. 371.

Mark Ward, *Virtual Organisms: The Startling World of Artificial Life*, London, Pan Books, 2000.

Bill Joy, 'Why the Future Doesn't Need Us', *Wired*, April 2000.

Lynn Margulis and Dorion Sagan, *Microcosmos*, Berkeley and London, University of California Press, 1997.

George Santayana, *Winds of Doctrine, and Platonism and the Spiritual Life*, New York, Harper and Brothers, 1957.

6 AS IT IS

Joseph Brodsky, 'Wooing the Inanimate: Four Poems by Thomas Hardy', in *On Grief and Reason: Essays*, London, Penguin, 1995.

Joseph Conrad, *Nostromo*, London, J. M. Dent and Sons, 1947.

For Wyndham Lewis's brilliant, if at times perverse, attack on the idea of progress, see his *The Demon of Progress in the Arts*, London, Methuen, 1954. I owe my knowledge of this book to the late Isaiah Berlin. I discuss time-worship in modern liberalism in 'Santayana and the Critique of Liberalism', *Post-liberalism: Studies in Political Thought*, London and New York, Routledge, 1993.

For a brilliant application of pagan ethics to contemporary statesmanship, see Robert D. Kaplan, *Warrior Politics: Why Leadership Demands a Pagan Ethos*, New York, Random House, 2002.

See Colin M. Turnbull, *Wayward Servants: The Two Worlds of the African Pygmies*, London, Eyre and Spottiswoode, 1966.

Robert Graves, 'Sisyphus', *The Greek Myths*, Vol. 1, London, Penguin Books, 1955.

George Santayana, *Winds of Doctrine, and Platonism and the Spiritual Life*, New York, Harper and Brothers, 1957.

INDEX

PERMISSION ACKNOWLEDGEMENTS

Grateful acknowledgement is made for permission to reprint the following material:

'Christ on the Cross', translated by Alexander Coleman, copyright © 1999 by Maria Kodama; translation copyright © 1999 by Alexander Coleman, from *Selected Poems* by Jorge Luis Borges, edited by Alexander Coleman. Used by permission of Viking Penguin, a division of Penguin Group (USA) Inc.

Poems from Robinson Jeffers: *The Collected Poetry of Robinson Jeffers, Volume 2: 1928–1938*, edited by Tim Hunt, copyright © 1938, renewed © 1966 by Donnan Jeffers and Garth Jeffers. All rights reserved.

Thirteen lines from *The Iliad of Homer*, translated by Richmond Lattimore, copyright © 1951 by The University of Chicago, courtesy of The University of Chicago Press.

One line from 'To Robinson Jeffers', from *Visions from San Francisco Bay*, by Czeslaw Milosz, translated by Richard Lourie.

Excerpt from *Poems of Fernando Pessoa*, by Fernando Pessoa, translation copyright © 1998 by Edwin Honig and Susan M. Brown. Reprinted by permission of City Lights Books.

Made in the USA
Middletown, DE
28 October 2020